MOON METRO
SEATTLE

CONTENTS

INTRODUCTION
HOW TO USE THIS BOOK, p. IV
INTRODUCTION TO SEATTLE, p. VI

A DAY IN SEATTLE
THE BEST OF SEATTLE, p. X
SEATTLE BY BIKE, p. XII
ARTISTIC SEATTLE, p. XIV

NEIGHBORHOOD MAPS

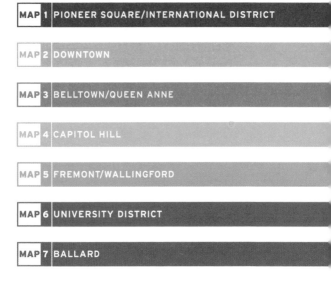

MAP 1 PIONEER SQUARE/INTERNATIONAL DISTRICT

MAP 2 DOWNTOWN

MAP 3 BELLTOWN/QUEEN ANNE

MAP 4 CAPITOL HILL

MAP 5 FREMONT/WALLINGFORD

MAP 6 UNIVERSITY DISTRICT

MAP 7 BALLARD

AVALON TRAVEL

SIGHTS, p. 1

RESTAURANTS, p. 19

NIGHTLIFE, p. 35

SHOPS, p. 45

ARTS AND LEISURE, p. 59

MUSEUMS AND GALLERIES, p. 60
PERFORMING ARTS, p. 67
RECREATION, p. 73

HOTELS, p. 79

CITY ESSENTIALS, p. 87
STREET INDEX, p. 93
INDEX, p. 98

HOW TO USE THIS BOOK

MAP SECTION

- We've divided Seattle into seven distinct areas. Each area has been assigned a color, used on the map itself and in easy-to-spot map number indicators throughout the listings.

- The maps show the location of every listing in the book, using the icon that indicates what type of listing it is (sight, restaurant, etc.) and the listing's locator number.

- The coordinates (in color) indicate the specific grid that the listing is located in. The black number is the listing's locator number. The page number directs you to the listing's full description.

LISTINGS SECTION

- Listings are organized into six sections:

  ⊙ SIGHTS

  ⊛ RESTAURANTS

  ⊗ NIGHTLIFE

  ⊜ SHOPS

  ⊘ ARTS AND LEISURE

  ⊕ HOTELS

- Within each section, listings are organized by which map they are located in, then in alphabetical order.

MAP 1 PIONEER SQUARE/INTERNATIONAL DIS

CAFÉ PALOMA QUICK BITES • MEDITERRANEAN $
Some things are more pleasing in miniature – like this tiny Pioneer Square retreat that serves pressed panini and freshly squeezed orange juice. While eating, enjoy the pedestrian hustle of the streets or the rotating art exhibits hung on the colorful walls.
MAP 1 A2 ⊙ 4 93 YESLER WAY
206-405-1920

CHINA GATE AFTER HOURS • DIM SUM $$
Dim sum carts are easy to find in the International District, but China Gate offers a special dumpling experience. In addition to all the pork and seafood favorites, many veggies, like eggplant and Chinese greens, get great treatment here.
MAP 1 C5 ⊙ 37 516 7TH AVE. S.
206-624-1730

GRAND CENTRAL BAKING COMPANY QUICK BITES • SANDWICHES $
This old-fashioned brick building plays a big part in the Northwest's artisanal bread history. Since 1972, the Grand Central has supplied restaurants around the city with exceptional loaves and has created great sandwiches, like the basil egg salad and the focaccia with havarti and roasted vegetables, for its Pioneer Square patrons.
MAP 1 B2 ⊙ 11 214 1ST AVE. S.
206-622-3644

MANEKI QUICK BITES • JAPANESE $$
Although its origins are lost in legend, Seattle's oldest Japanese restaurant celebrated its 100th anniversary in 2004 and retains a traditional atmosphere with bilingual menus and tatami-floored back rooms. The food offerings include fresh sushi and remarkable appetizer specials, such as the tempura-fried smelt and the scallop and mushroom sautée.
MAP 1 B5 ⊙ 28 304 6TH AVE. S.
206-622-2631

SALUMI HOT SPOT • DELI $
Whenever it's open, Armandino Batali's bowling lane of a space is packed with customers clamoring for his oxtail sandwiches and house-crafted salamis. They gather around the deli's big single table and chat with tablemates, whom they know share their devotion to great meat.
MAP 1 B3 ⊙ 23 309 3RD AVE. S.
206-621-8772

SHANGHAI GARDEN BUSINESS • CHINESE $$
The decor here may need an update, but Shanghai Garden's food stands out among the many Chinese restaurants in the International District. Along with all the standards, there are also more unusual items like the wonderful black moss and bamboo fungus soup, the signature hand-shaved barley noodles, and high-nutrition fried brown rice.
MAP 1 C5 ⊙ 36 524 6TH AVE. S.
206-625-1689

20 MOON METRO

1. Scan the map to see what listings are in the area you want to explore. Use the directory to find out the name and page number for each listing.

2. Read the listings to find the specific place you want to visit. Use the map information at the bottom of each listing to find the listing's exact location.

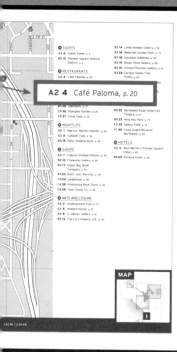

O SIGHTS
A3 6 Smith Tower, p. 3
B2 12 Pioneer Square Historic District, p. 2

O RESTAURANTS
A2 4 Café Paloma, p. 20

A2 4 Café Paloma, p. 20

C5 36 Shanghai Garden, p. 20
C5 37 China Gate, p. 20

O NIGHTLIFE
A2 1 Marcus' Martini Heaven, p. 36
A3 8 Catwalk Club, p. 36
B3 15 Fenix Underground, p. 36

O SHOPS
A3 7 Laguna Vintage Pottery, p. 44
B2 10 Fireworks Gallery, p. 44
B3 17 Elliott Bay Book Company, p. 44
B3 20 Bud's Jazz Records, p. 44
C4 34 Uwajimaya, p. 44
C4 35 Kinokuniya Book Store, p. 44
C6 38 Tsue Chong Co., p. 44

O ARTS AND LEISURE
A2 2 Underground Tour, p. 73
A3 5 Howard House, p. 61
A4 9 G. Gibson Gallery, p. 61
B2 13 Flury & Company, Ltd., p. 60

B2 14 Linda Hodges Gallery, p. 61
B3 16 Waterfall Garden Park, p. 73
B3 18 Davidson Galleries, p. 60
B3 19 Bryan Ohno Gallery, p. 60
B3 21 Grover/Thurston Gallery, p. 60
B3 22 Carolyn Staley Fine Prints, p. 60

B5 32 Northwest Asian American Theatre, p. 67
B5 33 Hing Hay Park, p. 73
E3 39 Safeco Field, p. 73
F1 40 Coast Guard Museum Northwest, p. 60

O HOTELS
A2 3 Best Western Pioneer Square Hotel, p. 80
B5 29 Panama Hotel, p. 81

MAP
1

1.52 MI / 2.45 KM

MAP KEY

Major Sights	★
Monorail	Ⓜ
Shopping District	―――
Stairs	∥∥∥∥∥∥∥∥∥
Pedestrian Street	
Adjacent Map Boundaries	SEE MAP 1 ▷
Streetcar	Ⓢ
Carpool Lane	◆
Burke-Gilman Trail	··············

SECTION ICONS

O SIGHTS

R RESTAURANTS

N NIGHTLIFE

S SHOPS

A ARTS AND LEISURE

H HOTELS

RESTAURANTS

SALUMI   TAKOHACHI

TAKOHACHI
A happy octopus...
where they car...
cod katsutake, cr...
sushi, but do e...
young Japanese...
[map] B5 ☐ 24

ZEITGEIST C...
Zeitgeist is on...
exposed brick,...
coffee, it make...
exhibits and fil...
[map] B3 ☐ 26

CAFÉ PALOMA   *QUICK BITES • MEDITERRANEAN*   **$**
Some things are more pleasing in miniature – like this tiny Pioneer Square retreat that serves pressed *panini* and freshly squeezed orange juice. While eating, enjoy the pedestrian hustle of the streets or the rotating art exhibits hung on the colorful walls.

MAP 1 A2 **R** 4   93 YESLER WAY
206-405-1920

ALEXANDRI...
Alexandria's ch...
cooking up entrées like shrimp jambalaya and smothered pork with...
a side of black-eyed peas and dessert classics like sweet potato pie...
The separate bar is very popular with the after-work crowd.
[map] B2 ☐ 13   2020 2ND AVE.
206-374-3700

Use the **MAP NUMBER, COLOR GRID COORDINATES**, and **BLACK LOCATOR NUMBER** to find the exact location of every listing in the book.

BROOKLYN SEAFOOD, STEAK & OYSTER
HOUSE   *BUSINESS • PACIFIC NORTHWEST* $$$
Highly favored among Seattle's business population, the Brooklyn is...
a classic steakhouse with some of the best chops in town. The oys...
ter bar features more than a dozen varieties, and the martinis are...
everything you'd expect.
[map] B4 ☐ 65   1212 2ND AVE.
206-224-7000

CAMPAGNE   *ROMANTIC • FRENCH* $$$
Chef Daisley Gordon regularly dips into the bounty of the market for

21

INTRODUCTION TO
SEATTLE

Contrary to popular belief, it does not always rain in Seattle. Most days may be overcast – and admittedly often misty – between October and May, but the truth of the matter is that New York averages more inches of rainfall per year than Seattle does. But as much as the people here complain about the weather, it's just as important to Seattle's character as the Space Needle. After all, without all the drizzle, Bill Gates may never have spe nt all those hours indoors fiddling with his computer, Starbucks may never have been inspired to steam its first cappuccino, and the city's flourishing evergreens may never have made it past their first sprout.

In fact, water is just about everywhere you look in Seattle, whether it's raining or not. Elliott Bay, Lake Union, and Lake Washington pour out across the city's scattered land-scape, making it hard to get anywhere without crossing a bridge or boarding a ferry. Even the surrounding peaks of the Cascades, Olympics, and Mount Rainier are snow-capped with frozen moisture. On a summer day, down-town's skyscrapers climb up against a majestic backdrop of frosty whites, grassy greens, and ocean blues. They don't call it the Emerald City for nothing.

All this natural beauty has consequently turned Seattleites into some of the most outdoorsy folks in the United States, with first-rate skiing, hiking, and boat-ing right in Seattle's own backyard. It's no wonder that earth-loving superstores like REI and Eddie Bauer got their starts here, subsequently setting the city's dress

SEATTLE'S ASIAN AMERICAN COMMUNITY

In the late 1800s and early 1900s, hopeful Chinese, Japanese, and Korean immigrants, among others, came to Seattle by the shipload, due to the city's proximity to the Pacific Rim. Today Asian Americans are Seattle's largest minority group. In fact, the International District (a.k.a. "the I.D.") was even the birthplace for Wa Chong Co., the United States' first Asian-owned manufacturing business.

The community's influence can be seen everywhere, from Chinese American Gary Locke's popular run as governor between 1997 and 2004 to Japanese baseball player Ichiro Suzuki's recent success as a superstar for the Mariners. Check out the Wing Luke Asian Museum for a detailed account of Seattle's Asian American history, and browse the isles at Uwajimaya – the Pacific Northwest's largest indoor Asian market – for a peek into Seattle's Asian American community of today.

code somewhere between natural and casual. Even when attending a high-end show at one of Seattle's many vibrant theaters, people dressed in flannels and fleeces are just as common as those in ties and gowns. In fact, Seattle native Bill Gates reportedly goes to work here in jeans.

That's not to say Seattle doesn't have an urban edge. Just take a walk through Capitol Hill, Fremont, or Belltown, and you'll quickly see Seattle's inclination for cosmopolitan boutiques, bistros, and, of course, cafés. The city that gave the world Starbucks has more coffeehouses per capita than any other place in the United States, a statistic that keeps its citizens highly caffeinated and truly "sleepless in Seattle." But Starbucks isn't the only local company keeping the city wired; Microsoft's nearby headquarters have undoubtedly fueled Seattle's passion for all things digital, making laptops as abundant as lattes.

Still, despite all of its modernizations, some of Seattle's most celebrated aspects are the ones that have assuredly stayed the same: The Space Needle still has its grand panoramic views, Pioneer Square still has its historic red-brick buildings, and Pike Place Market still has its fresh

Pacific salmon. Even with all the futuristic skyscrapers and Palm Pilots, Seattle still sits against the same gorgeous background of age-old mountain peaks and ocean waters. Not even a rainy day could muddle Seattle's many distinct charms. In fact, a little drizzle now and then only helps to nourish them all the more.

HISTORY

The first European settlers in Seattle arrived to – what else? – wind and rain. In 1851, Seattle founder Arthur Denny and his associates first landed on stormy Alki Point, but they later moved inland to the east side of Elliott Bay, present-day downtown. After befriending the local Native American tribes who inhabited the area, settlers named the city Seattle after Chief Sealth of the Duwamish tribe.

Seattle grew to become a medium-sized lumber town until the Great Fire of 1889 blazed through the city's entire business district. It wasn't a total loss, however, since stronger brick buildings – many still standing in Pioneer Square today – replaced much of the damage. In 1897, the Klondike Gold Rush streamed tons of big spenders through Seattle, swelling the city's revenue and population. By the time Boeing Airplane Company established itself here in 1916, Seattle was well on its way to becoming a U.S. metropolis.

Still, much of Seattle's urban development came in the late-20th century, particularly after the attention it got for hosting the 1962 World's Fair. Seattle later became an epicenter for Microsoft and other growing dot-com companies in the '80s and '90s, but when a recession hit in 2000, many computer corporations buckled. Although the Nisqually Earthquake and Boeing's corporate move to Chicago hit Seattle hard in 2001, the city nevertheless has been on the slow road to recovery ever since.

THE MONORAIL'S PAST – AND FUTURE

One of the city's additions for the 1962 World's Fair (along with the Space Needle), the Seattle Center Monorail was initially built to connect the fairgrounds and downtown. Many were skeptical that the monorail would make back its $3.5 million in costs, but it exceeded expectations by carrying some eight million passengers in its first six months. In fact, the monorail's popularity peaked when it was featured in the Elvis Presley movie *It Happened at the World's Fair.* More recently in 2004, however, one of the two trains burst into flames, prompting immediate evacuation by the Seattle Fire Department. Luckily no one was injured, but the future of this historic transport doesn't look good: With the approval of the Monorail Green Line Project, which is set to connect several Seattle neighborhoods, the Seattle Center Monorail will eventually have to be torn down.

SPACE NEEDLE

PIONEER SQUARE
HISTORIC DISTRICT

THE BEST OF
SEATTLE

To see the best that Seattle has to offer, you could kick back and let a tour bus do all the work, but this is a think-for-yourself city, where being your own leader can get you as far as your own billion-dollar software company. So with enough caffeine, you can tackle many of Seattle's major sights in one day. Here's one way to take on the Emerald City in 24 hours, but you probably won't make it very far unless you start with a cue from the locals: Make that latte a double.

1 Begin your day with a leisurely roam through **Pike Place Market (p. 4).** Not only can you munch your way through the bakeries and produce stands for breakfast, but you can also check out the world's first Starbucks.

2 Take the Pike Place Hillclimb down to the waterfront, and catch a mid-morning ride on a **Washington State Ferry (p. 7).** The views from the water are some of the best in the city.

3 After your watery jaunt, spend some time exploring the waterfront before hopping the **Waterfront Streetcar (p. 74)** to Occidental Park and the Pioneer Square area.

4 Grab lunch at the **Grand Central Baking Company (p. 20).** Forget counting carbs: These loaves are some of the tastiest in the city.

5 After lunch, poke around the **Pioneer Square Historic District (p. 2).** For a different perspective, take the **Underground Tour (p. 73),** a below-street-level peek into Seattle's frontier-era past.

6 Time to refuel? Enjoy an afternoon cappuccino – and some prime Seattle café culture – at **Zeitgeist Coffee (p. 21).** For many Seattleites, the espresso here is as good as it gets.

7 Catch a bus (or walk, if your caffeine kicks in) to the **Central Library (p. 3).** Simply check out the architecture, or take a look inside.

8 A few blocks up, downtown's shopping district holds the **Nordstrom (p. 48)** headquarters and upscale **Pacific Place (p. 49).**

9 Jump on the monorail to the Seattle Center, and test your musical IQ at the **Experience Music Project (p. 8),** conveniently open till 8 P.M. in the summer.

10 Dine in 360-degree style at the rotating **Sky City (p. 28)** restaurant on top of the **Space Needle (p. 10).** Be sure to make reservations beforehand.

11 Hail a cab back to Pike Place, and end your day at the **Pink Door (p. 37),** one of Seattle's oldest – and most charming – martini bars. As in the morning, make that drink a double – you deserve it.

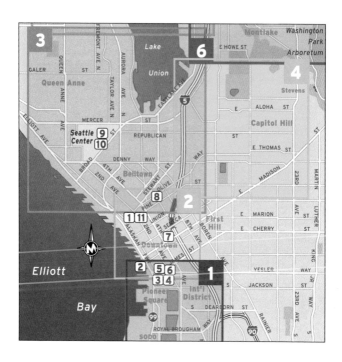

UNIVERSITY OF
WASHINGTON

GAS WORKS PARK

WOODLAND PARK ZOO

SEATTLE
BY BIKE

It may seem ironic that a city known for its rainy weather is also known for its great outdoors, but once you start taking in Seattle's natural beauty, you'll no doubt thank the clouds for nurturing all the greenery. And since Seattle has continuously been rated one of the nation's top cycling cities, the best way to experience its open-air offerings is on two wheels. You can fill a whole day with scenic stops, so grab your helmet and start peddling.

1 Rent a bike at **Gregg's Green Lake Cycle (p. 77),** just north of Wallingford. Gregg's is the top spot in the city for rentals of all kinds, so you're definitely in good hands. Afterward, test out your bike around **Green Lake (p. 77).**

2 Make your way south to the **Burke Museum of Natural History and Culture (p. 14).** This museum may be indoors, but it's all about getting in touch with nature.

3 Back outside, coast around the **University of Washington (p. 16)** campus. Keep in mind that riding is prohibited during class breaks.

4 Grab lunch at the **Aqua Verde Paddle Club & Café (p. 31),** which serves some very tasty seafood

tacos. Try to nab one of the tables on the deck overlooking Portage Bay.

5 Climb on your bike again, and follow the **Burke-Gilman Trail (p. 75)** along Lake Union (you can access it on Brooklyn Avenue NE, near NE Pacific Street). Stop at **Gas Works Park (p. 76)** for stellar views of downtown and the houseboats on Lake Union.

6 Continue along the Burke-Gilman till you get to **Fremont (p. 54),** one of Seattle's funkiest neighborhoods. Browse the unique shops, and catch your breath at one of the many cafés.

7 Two-wheel it straight up Fremont Avenue North to the **Woodland Park Zoo (p. 13).** Lock up your bike, and get acquainted with the park's gorillas and elephants.

8 Take 50th Street westbound to Ballard. Make sure to ride along historic Ballard Avenue on your way to the **Hiram M. Chittenden Locks (p. 17).** Watch the boats get pumped in and out, and keep an eye out for jumping salmon.

9 For dinner, fill up on comfort food at **Hattie's Hat (p. 33).**

10 If there's still daylight, peddle to nearby **Discovery Park (p. 18)** to scope views and rest your legs – that is, until you have to bike back.

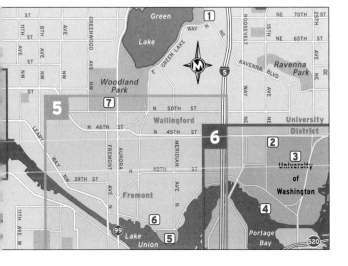

SEATTLE ART MUSEUM   VOLUNTEER PARK   SEATTLE ASIAN ART MUSEUM

ARTISTIC
SEATTLE

Art is just about everywhere you look in Seattle, whether it's nailed to a street corner or tattooed on someone's back. In fact, Seattle has more arts-related organizations per capita than any other city in the United States, according to a recent study. Theaters, concert halls, and museums are about as common as coffee bars here, and local neighborhoods like Fremont have enough freestanding art to warrant self-guided tours. Take a day to get in touch with Seattle's creative side, and keep your camera ready.

☐ Start your day browsing the granddaddy of them all: the **Seattle Art Museum (p. 6).** It's easy to find: Just keep an eye out for the 48-foot metal man hammering away at the sidewalk.

② Walk or take a bus along 1st Avenue to Pioneer Square, where you'll find the highest concentration of local art galleries. Make sure to check out the Chihuly glasswork at the **Foster/White Gallery (p. 60).**

③ Take a cab to **Capitol Hill (p. 52),** and poke through the shops along Broadway, Pine, and Pike. Not only will you find plenty of creative boutiques on this street, but you'll also find plenty of creative outfits. For lunch, try a crusty sandwich from **Baguette Box (p. 28).**

④ Walk to **Volunteer Park (p. 75)** on top of the Hill, and catch some grand city views. Then, head into the **Seattle Asian Art Museum (p. 11)** to take in some early Ming Dynasty works.

⑤ While you're in the area, dip over to the **Lake View Cemetery (p. 12),** where you'll find the gravestones of martial artist Bruce Lee and his son Brandon.

⊙ SIGHTS

A2 **1** Woodland Park Zoo, p. 13

ⓡ RESTAURANTS

B4 **5** Asteroid Cafe, p. 30
B5 **8** Teahouse Kuan Yin, p. 31
B5 **9** Kabul Afghan Cuisine, p. 31
D2 **13** Roxy's Deli, p. 31
D3 **24** Jai Thai, p. 30
D3 **25** 35th St. Bistro, p. 31
D3 **28** Bandoleone, p. 30

ⓝ NIGHTLIFE

B4 **4** Beso del Sol, p. 42
C3 **11** Fabulous Buckaroo Tavern, p. 42
D2 **12** The George & Dragon Pub, p. 43
D2 **15** Tost, p. 43
D2 **17** Triangle Lounge, p. 43

ⓢ SHOPS

B5 **6** Wide World Books & Maps, p. 56
B5 **7** Wallingford Center, p. 55
B6 **10** Open Books: A Poem Emporium, p. 55
D2 **16** Bitters Co., p. 54
D2 **18** Burnt Sugar, p. 54
D2 **19** Les Amis, p. 55
D3 **20** Fremont, p. 54

D3 **21** Deluxe Junk, p. 54
D3 **22** Enexile, p. 54
D3 **23** Essenza, p. 54
D3 **26** Lola Pop, p. 55
D3 **27** Sonic Boom Records, p. 55
D3 **29** Dandelion Botanical Company, p. 54
E4 **31** Gasworks Park Kite Shop, p. 54

ⓐ ARTS AND LEISURE

A3 **2** Woodland Park Rose Garden, p. 76
D2 **14** Fremont Public Art Walk, p. 75
D3 **30** History House, p. 65
E5 **32** Burke-Gilman Trail, p. 75
E5 **33** Gas Works Park, p. 76
F4 **34** Lake Union Houseboats, p. 76

ⓗ HOTELS

A3 **3** Chelsea Station on the Park, p. 86

MAP

UNIVERSITY DISTRICT

Primarily a college quarter, the U District, as locals call it, centers around the University of Washington and its 40,000 scholars. There are, of course, plenty of others making use of this energetic area, but the majority of the inhabitants here tend to be fresh-faced twentysomethings sporting Go Huskies! T-shirts and lugging around overstuffed bookbags. Still, the nearby Burke Museum and Washington Park Arboretum both remain relatively student-free, but that's probably just because those hard-working pupils are too busy studying – or partying.

Not surprisingly, the immediate area surrounding UW (pronounced "U Dub") has been adjusted to fit the needs – and wallets – of its students: Cheap ethnic eats, second-hand record shops, and college-centric sports bars flood nearby University Way (a.k.a. "The Ave"). On the other side of the school, the University Village offers a much more mall-like shopping experience, featuring chain stores like the Gap and Banana Republic. The campus itself, however, is timeless: With its Romanesque and Gothic Revival structures, it gives off the kind of historic feeling you might expect from a medieval European villa – that is, if it weren't for all the Abercrombie-clad undergrads.

MAP 6 UNIVERSITY DISTRICT

Lake
Union

SEE MAP 6

E GARFIELD ST

E GARFIELD ST

Lake View

Cemetery 2 ★

E GALER ST

Conservatory

St. Mark's
Episcopal
Cathedral

Volunteer 3

★4 Harvard–Belmont
Landmark District

E HIGHLAND DR

Park

SEATTLE ASIAN
ART MUSEUM 7

H 8

STEVENS

HIGHLAND DR

E PROSPECT ST

PROSPECT ST

E WARD ST

ALOHA

E VALLEY ST H 9

ROY

MERCER

REPUBLICAN

S 13

HARRISON

S 14

THOMAS

15 R

H 16

CAPITOL
HILL

E THOMAS ST

E JOHN ST

E JANSEN CT

E GLEN ST

DENNY WAY

Lincoln
Res

Bobby
Morris
Playfield

HOWELL

17

OLIVE

Seattle Central
Community College

19 H

OLIVE

20

21

N

N N

30 31

18 N

41

22 23

S

24 25 26

R

27 28 29

Seattle Central
Community College

33

N 32

34

A,N

40

36

A

N 39

A 37

38 R

PINE

44 45

A

PIKE

N 42

N 43

COCA

UNION

N 46

S 12

SEE MAP 3

SEE MAP 2

0   0.1 KM   0   0.1 MI   DISTANCE ACROSS MAP: 1.63 MI / 2.6 KM

MAP 4 CAPITOL HILL

MAP 6

⭐ SIGHTS

D3 **28** Experience Music Project, p. 8
D3 **31** Space Needle, p. 10
E3 **43** Pacific Science Center, p. 9

🍴 RESTAURANTS

A2 **5** Ototo Sushi, p. 26
A2 **6** Hilltop Ale House, p. 25
A6 **8** Serafina, p. 27
B2 **10** Sapphire Kitchen & Bar, p. 27
D2 **20** Tup Tim Thai, p. 28
D3 **30** Sky City, p. 28
E2 **41** Afrikando, p. 24
F2 **47** Waterfront, p. 28
F3 **49** El Gaucho, p. 25
F3 **52** Macrina Bakery & Cafe, p. 26
F3 **53** Lampreia, p. 25
F3 **54** Shiro's, p. 27
F3 **59** Cascadia Restaurant, p. 24
F3 **61** Flying Fish, p. 25
F3 **62** Apartment Bistro, p. 24
F4 **65** Mistral, p. 26
F4 **66** Restaurant Zoë, p. 26
F4 **67** Saito's Japanese Café & Bar, p. 27
F4 **68** Brasa, p. 24
F4 **72** Assaggio Ristorante, p. 24
F4 **73** Lola, p. 26
F4 **74** Dahlia Lounge, p. 25

🌙 NIGHTLIFE

C5 **18** BluWater Bistro, p. 38
D2 **22** Mirabeau Room, p. 39
D3 **34** Element, p. 38
D6 **39** Café Venus and the Mars Bar, p. 38
E2 **40** Tini Bigs, p. 39
E6 **46** Graceland, p. 39
F3 **50** Cyclops, p. 38
F3 **55** Rendezvous, p. 39
F3 **57** Shorty's Coney Island, p. 39
F3 **58** The Crocodile Cafe, p. 38
F3 **63** Club Medusa, p. 38
F4 **64** Tula's Restaurant and Nightclub, p. 40

🛍 SHOPS

A1 **1** Rhinestone Rosie, p. 52
A2 **2** The Teacup, p. 52
A2 **3** A Salon Day Spa Boutique, p. 52
A2 **4** Queen Anne Mail & Dispatch, p. 51
B2 **9** Queen Anne Books, p. 51

B2 **11** La Femme, p. 51
B2 **12** Queen Anne, p. 51
F3 **48** Chartreuse International, p. 51

🎭 ARTS AND LEISURE

A4 **7** NW Outdoor Center, p. 75
C1 **13** Kerry Park, p. 75
C2 **14** On the Boards, p. 69
C4 **15** Kenmore Air, p. 74
C5 **16** Summer Nights at South Lake Union, p. 70
C5 **17** The Center for Wooden Boats, p. 63
D2 **23** Seattle Repertory Theatre, p. 70
D2 **24** Intiman Theatre, p. 68
D2 **26** Key Arena, p. 68
D3 **27** The Children's Museum, p. 63
D3 **29** Science Fiction Museum and Hall of Fame, p. 64
D3 **32** Book-It Repertory Theatre, p. 68
D3 **33** Marion Oliver McCaw Hall, p. 68
D3 **35** Ride the Ducks, p. 75
D4 **36** Center on Contemporary Art (CoCA), p. 63
D4 **37** 911 Media Arts Center, p. 69
D5 **38** Consolidated Works, p. 68
E3 **42** Seattle Children's Theatre, p. 69
E4 **44** Teatro Zinzanni, p. 70
E5 **45** Re-Bar, p. 69
F3 **56** Roq La Rue Gallery, p. 64
F4 **69** Seattle Cinerama Theatre, p. 69
F4 **70** Dimitriou's Jazz Alley, p. 68

🏨 HOTELS

C6 **19** Silver Cloud Inn-Lake Union, p. 83
D2 **21** MarQueen Hotel, p. 83
D2 **25** Mediterranean Inn, p. 83
F3 **51** The Ace Hotel, p. 83
F3 **60** The Edgewater, p. 83
F4 **71** Warwick Hotel, p. 84
F4 **73** Hotel Ändra, p. 83
F5 **75** The Westin Seattle, p. 84
F5 **76** Vance Hotel, p. 83

MAP

3

CAPITOL HILL

Pioneers may have envisioned the state capital here, but today there's not a three-piece suit in sight. Instead, expect a grunge-influenced dress code of body art, lip piercings, and multihued hairstyles. Capitol Hill is Seattle's capital of counterculture, where even the almighty Starbucks loses ground to independent coffeehouses, and Seattle's own Nordstrom wouldn't have a chance against the vintage boutiques. Browse through fetish fashion shops and tattoo parlors along bustling Broadway, then test your tango and waltzing skills across the street's brass dancing steps – that is, if you don't get interrupted too many times by aggressive panhandlers in this area.

Aside from all the excitement on Broadway, there are two other main sectors on the Hill: On top sits Volunteer Park, home of the Seattle Asian Art Museum, where locals go to get some fresh air, throw Frisbees, and even sunbathe when the weather calls for it. Back down on the south side of Broadway lies the Pike/Pine corridor, home base for much of the Hill's after-dark action, as well as Seattle's highest concentration of gay and lesbian bars. And although much of Capitol Hill has been subject to a good amount of commercialization, it's definitely not showing any signs of losing that alternative edge – it's still the only place in the city where you can run into a drag queen shopping at Fred Meyer.

MAP 4 CAPITOL HILL

SEE MAP 5

QUEEN ANNE

Lake

Union

Kerry Park

South Lake Union Park

Repertory Theatre
Intiman Theatre

Seattle Center

EXPERIENCE MUSIC PROJECT

Key Arena
Int'l Fountain
The Children's Museum
Seattle Children's Theatre

SPACE NEEDLE

PACIFIC SCIENCE CENTER

Cascade Playground

Denny Park

Myrtle Edwards Park

Elliott

Bay

BELLTOWN

Regrade Park

Paramount Theatre

Pacific Place
Nordstrom

The Moore Theatre

Westlake Center

SEE MAP 2

Convention Center

CLIPPER

DISTANCE ACROSS MAP: 1.93 MI / 3.1 KM

0   0.1 KM   0   0.1 MI

MAP 3 BELLTOWN/QUEEN ANNE

☆ SIGHTS

C2 **33** Pike Place Market, p. 4
D2 **58** Seattle Aquarium, p. 5
D3 **60** Seattle Art Museum, p. 6
D5 **70** Central Library, p. 3
F3 **80** Washington State Ferries, p. 7

® RESTAURANTS

A4 **5** Oceanaire Seafood Room, p. 23
B2 **13** Alexandria's on Second, p. 21
B2 **19** Le Pichet, p. 22
C2 **34** Campagne, p. 21
C2 **38** Pan Africa, p. 23
C2 **41** Chez Shea, p. 22
C2 **42** Matt's in the Market, p. 23
C2 **45** Place Pigalle, p. 23
C3 **48** Wild Ginger, p. 24
C4 **55** The Georgian, p. 22
D4 **65** Brooklyn Seafood, Steak & Oyster House, p. 21
D4 **66** Sazerac, p. 23
D4 **67** Troiani, p. 23
D5 **68** Earth & Ocean, p. 22
E4 **76** The Library Bistro, p. 22
E4 **78** Metropolitan Grill, p. 23
E5 **79** Crow, p. 22

® NIGHTLIFE

A1 **1** Bada Lounge, p. 36
B2 **17** Nitelite, p. 36
B2 **18** Virginia Inn, p. 37
B2 **23** The Pink Door, p. 37
C2 **43** Zig Zag Café, p. 37
C2 **44** Alibi Room, p. 36
C3 **46** The Showbox, p. 37
C3 **47** The Triple Door, p. 37
F4 **81** Contour, p. 36

® SHOPS

A4 **2** Nordstrom, p. 48
A4 **3** Twist, p. 50
A4 **4** Pacific Place, p. 49
A4 **7** Flora and Henri, p. 47
B2 **15** J. Gilbert Footwear, p. 48
B2 **16** Opus 204, p. 48
B2 **21** Isadora's Antiques, p. 48
B2 **22** Zebraclub, p. 50
B2 **24** White Horse, p. 50
B3 **27** Ummelina, p. 50
B3 **28** Borders Books and Music, p. 47
B4 **29** Sway & Cake, p. 49
C2 **34** Fini, p. 47
C2 **36** Alhambra, p. 47
C2 **37** M Coy Books, p. 48

C2 **39** Metsker Maps of Seattle, p. 48
C2 **40** Left Bank Books Collective, p. 48
C4 **50** Parfumerie Elizabeth George, p. 49
C4 **52** Fox's Gem Shop, p. 47
C4 **54** Jeri Rice, p. 48
D3 **63** Tulip, p. 49
E3 **74** Ped, p. 49
E3 **75** Ye Olde Curiosity Shop, p. 50

® ARTS AND LEISURE

A5 **9** Paramount Theatre, p. 68
A5 **10** Woodside-Braseth Gallery, p. 63
B2 **14** The Moore Theatre, p. 67
B3 **26** See Seattle Walking Tours, p. 74
B5 **32** A Contemporary Theatre, p. 67
C3 **49** Benaroya Hall, p. 67
C4 **51** The 5th Avenue Theatre, p. 67
C4 **53** Seattle Architecture Foundation Tours, p. 73
C6 **56** Town Hall Seattle, p. 68
D2 **57** Waterfront Streetcar, p. 74
D2 **59** Waterfront Park, p. 74
D3 **61** Soundbridge, p. 62
D3 **64** Benham Gallery, p. 62
E2 **72** Argosy Cruises, p. 73
E2 **73** Tillicum Village, p. 74

® HOTELS

A4 **6** The Paramount Hotel, p. 81
A5 **8** Grand Hyatt Seattle, p. 80
A5 **11** Summerfield Suites, p. 82
B1 **12** Seattle Marriott Waterfront, p. 82
B2 **20** Pensione Nichols, p. 81
B3 **25** Mayflower Park Hotel, p. 81
B4 **30** The Roosevelt Hotel, p. 82
B5 **31** Sheraton Seattle, p. 82
C2 **35** Inn at the Market, p. 81
C4 **55** Fairmont Olympic Hotel, p. 80
D3 **62** Inn at Harbor Steps, p. 81
D4 **66** Hotel Monaco, p. 80
D5 **68** W Hotel, p. 82
D5 **69** Hotel Vintage Park, p. 80
D5 **71** Renaissance Seattle Hotel, p. 82
E4 **77** Alexis Hotel, p. 80

MAP

BELLTOWN/QUEEN ANNE

Belltown, the primary birthplace of Seattle grunge, certainly doesn't look so grungy anymore. Once a low-income refuge for struggling artists and musicians, this urban enclave just north of downtown has become one of Seattle's most fashionable neighborhoods. Super-chic bistros, 21st-century lounges, and high-end condos have made over 1st and 2nd Avenues. Still, the grunge scene hasn't totally vanished: Piercings are just about as common here as Prada.

Farther north, Queen Anne is the city's highest hill and may be best known for its sprawling downtown and bay views. But this area also has its fair share of contemporary retailers. Lower Queen Anne (a.k.a. "Uptown"), at the bottom of the southern slope, features a metropolitan mix of funky bars and old-brick apartments, while Upper Queen Anne, sitting atop the hill north of Roy, lines Queen Anne Avenue with high-brow boutiques and Victorian homes.

Situated between Belltown and Queen Anne is the Seattle Center, home to such attractions as the Space Needle, Experience Music Project, and Pacific Science Center. As a hub of arts and culture events, it hosts big summer festivals like the Bite of Seattle, Folklife, and Bumbershoot. During these events, look out: Colossal crowds overtake the sidewalks around Belltown and Queen Anne.

MAP 3 BELLTOWN/QUEEN ANNE

MAP 2 DOWNTOWN

★ SIGHTS

A3 6 Smith Tower, p. 3
B2 12 Pioneer Square Historic District, p. 2

ℝ RESTAURANTS

A2 4 Café Paloma, p. 20
B2 11 Grand Central Baking Company, p. 20
B3 23 Salumi, p. 20
B3 26 Zeitgeist Coffee, p. 21
B5 28 Maneki, p. 20
B5 30 Takohachi, p. 21
C5 36 Shanghai Garden, p. 20
C5 37 China Gate, p. 20

ℕ NIGHTLIFE

A2 1 Marcus' Martini Heaven, p. 36
A3 8 Catwalk Club, p. 36
B3 15 Fenix Underground, p. 36

ⓢ SHOPS

A3 7 Laguna Vintage Pottery, p. 46
B2 10 Fireworks Gallery, p. 46
B3 17 Elliott Bay Book Company, p. 46
B3 20 Bud's Jazz Records, p. 46
C4 34 Uwajimaya, p. 46
C4 35 Kinokuniya Book Store, p. 46
C6 38 Tsue Chong Co., p. 46

Ⓐ ARTS AND LEISURE

A2 2 Underground Tour, p. 73
A3 5 Howard House, p. 61
A4 9 G. Gibson Gallery, p. 61
B2 13 Flury & Company, Ltd., p. 60

B2 14 Linda Hodges Gallery, p. 61
B3 16 Waterfall Garden Park, p. 73
B3 18 Davidson Galleries, p. 60
B3 19 Bryan Ohno Gallery, p. 60
B3 21 Grover/Thurston Gallery, p. 61
B3 22 Carolyn Staley Fine Prints, p. 60
B3 24 Seattle Metropolitan Police Museum, p. 61
B3 25 Foster/White Gallery, p. 60
B4 27 Greg Kucera Gallery, p. 61
B5 31 Wing Luke Asian Museum, p. 62
B5 32 Northwest Asian American Theatre, p. 67
B5 33 Hing Hay Park, p. 73
E3 39 Safeco Field, p. 73
F1 40 Coast Guard Museum Northwest, p. 60

ℍ HOTELS

A2 3 Best Western Pioneer Square Hotel, p. 80
B5 29 Panama Hotel, p. 80

DOWNTOWN

Downtown, with its low-rise jeans and high-rise sky-scrapers, is Seattle's bustling playground for ultra-stylish hipsters and overstressed CEOs. It's all cement and glass, but the city's dense urban core is, unquestionably, very much alive. Shops, restaurants, and theaters flood the sidewalks around 4th and 5th Avenues, while rows of rigid office buildings tower overhead. The Seattle Art Museum and Central Library add some heavy doses of culture to all the commerce and couture, as do two of Seattle's most sought-after tourist destinations: Pike Place Market and the waterfront.

In many ways, Pike Place Market has been the heart and soul of Seattle ever since it first opened in 1907. Overflowing with feisty produce vendors, knee-slappin' street performers, and tons of captivated tourists, the Market is definitely a far cry from a typical chain supermarket. After all, there aren't many grocery stores out there where people throw salmon around like it's a football. Just below the Market lies Seattle's waterfront, which offers spectacular views of Elliott Bay and downtown, as well as access to prominent seaside attractions like the Seattle Aquarium and the Washington State Ferries.

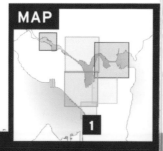

MAP

1

MAP 2 DOWNTOWN

6 Take a bus or catch a cab to quirky Fremont, and wander through the self-guided **Fremont Public Art Walk (p. 75)** – maps are available in street kiosks. Don't miss the Fremont Troll hiding under the Aurora Bridge.

7 Head down to Belltown, and dine at **Flying Fish (p. 25)**, one of Seattle's swankiest seafood joints. The plates themselves are works of art.

8 Take a walk around 1st Avenue for after-dinner drinks at the ultra-stylish **Bada Lounge (p. 36).** The contemporary decor is about as fashionable as the clientele.

9 There's no better way to finish off a day with the arts than with a show at the **Triple Door (p. 37),** a beautifully restored 1920s-era vaudeville theater.

PIONEER SQUARE/ INTERNATIONAL DISTRICT

In many ways, Pioneer Square – Seattle's oldest neighborhood – has not changed much since it was first constructed of iron, brick, and stone back in the late-19th century. Today it may have trendier restaurants, shops, and art galleries (mostly along 1st Avenue), but the real magic of Pioneer Square lies in its 20 city blocks of preserved redbrick history. The inhabitants, however, are anything but dated: The Square bustles with dot-com execs, art dealers, and amped-up sports fans, especially when the Mariners or Seahawks are playing. Bar-hoppers take over whenever the sun goes down, drawn by the area's booming nightlife scene – in fact, Pioneer Square clubs here even share a joint cover on weekends.

To the east, the International District, which locals refer to as "the I.D.," is a striking mix of Asian markets, herbal pharmacies, and fortune cookie factories. This area also reportedly has the most variety of ethnic groups of any other Chinatown in the United States, with Chinese, Japanese, Korean, Filipino, and Pacific Islander populations, among others, all sharing the same vicinity. And although it's true that the International District and Pioneer Square can seem slightly seedy at times, there's really nothing more to worry about than the occasional panhandler.

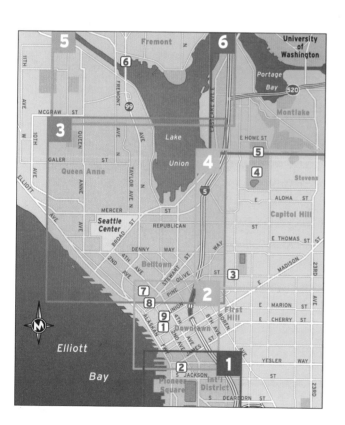

MAP 1 PIONEER SQUARE/INTERNATIONAL DISTRICT

⊕ SIGHTS

A3 12 Burke Museum of Natural History and Culture, p. 14
C3 20 University of Washington, p. 16
E5 26 Washington Park Arboretum, p. 15

⊛ RESTAURANTS

A2 7 Ugly Mug Cafe, p. 32
A2 8 Cedars, p. 32
A2 10 Than Brothers, p. 32
A6 14 Union Bay Cafe, p. 33
C2 19 Agua Verde Paddle Club & Cafe, p. 31
E4 25 Café Lago, p. 32

⊗ NIGHTLIFE

A1 1 Blue Moon Tavern, p. 43
A2 2 Tommy's Nightclub, p. 43
B2 15 Big Time Brewery & Alehouse, p. 43

⊗ SHOPS

A2 4 University Book Store, p. 57
A2 5 The Soap Box, p. 56
A2 11 Bulldog News, p. 56

⊘ ARTS AND LEISURE

A4 13 University Village, p. 57
Barnes & Noble, p. 56
Fran's Chocolates, p. 56
Mercer, p. 56
D1 21 Seattle Caviar Company, p. 56

B2 6 University District Public Art Tour, p. 76
B3 17 Henry Art Gallery, p. 65
B3 18 Meany Hall for the Performing Arts, p. 71
D4 22 University of Washington Waterfront Activities Center, p. 77
D4 23 Foster Island Walk, p. 76
D4 24 Museum of History & Industry (MOHAI), p. 65

⊗ HOTELS

A2 3 Best Western University Tower Hotel, p. 86
A2 9 Watertown, p. 86
B2 16 College Inn, p. 86

MAP

6

BALLARD

✪ SIGHTS
3 Hiram M. Chittenden Locks, p. 17

Ⓡ RESTAURANTS
1 Cafe Besalu, p. 33
2 Dandelion, p. 33
8 Market Street Grill, p. 33
10 Thaiku, p. 33
19 Hattie's Hat, p. 33

Ⓝ NIGHTLIFE
11 Sunset Tavern, p. 44
12 The People's Pub, p. 44
13 Tractor Tavern, p. 44
17 Portalis, p. 44
18 Old Town Alehouse, p. 43

Ⓢ SHOPS
4 Habitude at the Locks, p. 58
5 Archie McPhee, p. 57
6 Secret Garden Bookshop, p. 58
7 Scandinavian Gift Shop, p. 58
9 Ballard, p. 57
14 Olivine Atelier, p. 58
15 Lucca Great Finds, p. 58
16 Camelion Design, p. 57

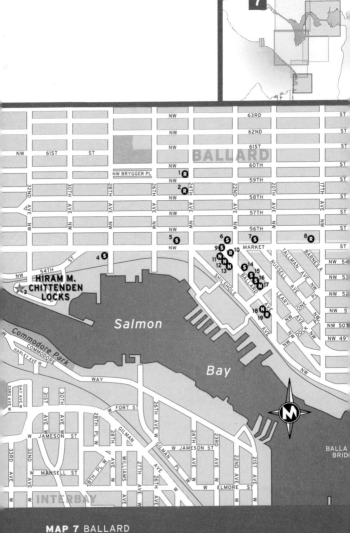

MAP 7

MAP 7 BALLARD

★ SIGHTS

Best place to gallery hop:
PIONEER SQUARE HISTORIC DISTRICT, p. 2

Most appealing library: **CENTRAL LIBRARY,** p. 3

Best place for fish: **PIKE PLACE MARKET,** p. 4

Best place to shake hands with a starfish:
SEATTLE AQUARIUM, p. 5

Best museum: **SEATTLE ART MUSEUM,** p. 6

Best cheap ride with a great view:
WASHINGTON STATE FERRIES, p. 7

Weirdest-looking building:
EXPERIENCE MUSIC PROJECT, p. 8

Best geek-out spot: **PACIFIC SCIENCE CENTER,** p. 9

Best 360-degree view: **SPACE NEEDLE,** p. 10

Best showcase of Asian art:
SEATTLE ASIAN ART MUSEUM, p. 11

Best animal-watching: **WOODLAND PARK ZOO,** p. 13

Best natural history museum:
**BURKE MUSEUM OF NATURAL HISTORY
AND CULTURE,** p. 14

Best place for a long, leisurely stroll:
WASHINGTON PARK ARBORETUM, p. 15

Best boat-viewing: **HIRAM M. CHITTENDEN LOCKS,** p. 17

Where to get in touch with nature: **DISCOVERY PARK,** p. 18

MAP 1 PIONEER SQUARE/INTERNATIONAL DISTRIC

PIONEER SQUARE HISTORIC DISTRICT

Built on a bog, Seattle's first business district was a lesson in respecting Mother Nature: At high tide, muddy streets would swallow children whole, and toilets flushed upward like geysers. The Great Fire of 1889, which was sparked when a glue pot in a furniture factory tipped over, was the best thing ever to happen to Pioneer Square. Not only did it eradicate a serious rat problem, it also prompted city planners to rebuild structures in stone and brick, and elevate them a story above the ruins. As you meander around the district, look downward for purple glass squares at intersections, skylights for the buried city.

Visitors can descend into preserved sections of this 1890s frontier town in an underground tour, where guides spice up colorful history and legitimate facts with one-liners and ghost tales. Aboveground, a walking tour yields other gems, such as the Klondike Gold Rush National Historical Park (the nation's smallest National Park), the National Fallen Firefighters Memorial, and Waterfall Garden Park.

The Historic District has a singular look, defined by the skillful restoration of Richardsonian Romanesque buildings designed by architect Elmer Fisher. Startups nabbed these hip addresses during the dot-com gold rush, but left a ghost town in their wake. In 2001, the Nisqually Earthquake dealt a second blow, leaving many office and retail spaces vacant due to major damage.

However, various specialty bookstores, Oriental rug galleries, and quirky shops continue to hold steady through boom and bust cycles, as do the it-crowd clubs and bars in the area. And the restaurants get better and more crowded by the day, handling fans from the Qwest and Safeco Fields, just to the south.

Recently, Pioneer Square has morphed into a gallery district with more than 30 art galleries and antique shops. A bit easier on your wallet are the sidewalk artists, who sell their wares along Occidental Avenue. On the first Thursday of every month, the galleries throw a collective block party, displaying the latest discoveries and providing buyers with free-flowing wine and cheese trays.

 MAP 1 B2 ⊕ 12   YESLER WAY TO S. KING ST. BTWN. ALASKAN WAY AND 3RD AVE.

PIONEER SQUARE
HISTORIC DISTRICT   SMITH TOWER   CENTRAL LIBRARY

SMITH TOWER

Seattle's first skyscraper, the 35-story Smith Tower, opened to public fanfare on July 4, 1914. The ornate decor and furnishings — a gift from the Empress of China — are dazzling, and a 360-degree outdoor viewing platform adds the beauty of Puget Sound.

 MAP 1 A3❂6   506 2ND AVE.
206-622-4004 (OBSERVATION DECK)

 MAP 2 DOWNTOWN

CENTRAL LIBRARY

Designed by world-renowned architect Rem Koolhaus, this spectacular glass and steel structure dominates 4th Avenue and adds a bit of character to an otherwise traditional cityscape.

Although a library might not normally be considered a tourist attraction, the design of this building is intended to draw people in from the street. The very modern architecture matches the library's other state-of-the-art features, such as the talking book repository outside and the automated book circulation system that ferries materials from floor to floor using a series of conveyor belts.

The austerity of the building exterior is completely lost in the brightly colored interior. The third-floor Living Room is a warm and inviting space where patrons may read their books or look up and see what awaits on the upper floors. The library's gift shop and coffee cart (of course!) are also located here.

A must-see on a library visit is the Books Spiral — a long, gently sloping ramp that winds through four floors of materials. This innovative design allows the

3

library's entire nonfiction collection to be accessed by anyone, without relying on stairs or elevators. The 10th floor holds the true reward: The view is spectacular, if not dizzying, and worth braving weekend crowds for. Tables and chairs allow a moment to slow down and enjoy views of the floors below, as well as the cityscape outside.

MAP 2 D5 ● 70 1000 4TH AVE. 206-386-4636
HOURS: MON.-WED. 10 A.M.-8 P.M., THURS.-SAT.
10 A.M.-6 P.M., SUN. 1-5 P.M.

PIKE PLACE MARKET

If it is possible to capture the essence of a city in one place, then Pike Place Market is Seattle's true soul. Its status approaches that of hallowed ground, sitting as it does on land where native tribes traded goods for centuries.

Today's market is a microeconomy of 700 or so butchers and fishmongers, produce and flower vendors, artists and craftspeople, restaurateurs and entrepreneurs. Visitors are immersed in the sights, sounds, and smells (both flowery and fishy) of the oldest continuously working market in the United States. The rich history of this cultural institution is evident in its cobblestone streets, restored brick buildings, and railroad-tie floors.

From horse-drawn produce carts in 1907, the market grew into a labyrinth of permanent stalls and shops on multiple levels and down hidden alleys. The Goodwin brothers built the Main Arcade in 1911, and for the next 30 years, waves of Sephardic Jews and other immigrants came here to build family businesses. After falling into neglect and disrepair in the 1960s, the market was slated to be demolished and replaced with a convention center and 4,000 parking stalls. But Victor Steinbrueck

SIDE WALKS

Walking along Seattle's magnificent waterfront is a happy way to spend the day. Starting at the Pike Place Market, you can easily walk down the Harbor Steps to the waterfront and enjoy the craft, food, and gift shops that await you. **Waterfront Park (p. 74)** offers beautiful views of Puget Sound along with benches and tables from which to admire them.

No trip to the waterfront would be complete without a stop at **Ye Olde Curiosity Shop (p. 50),** where you can see the world-famous Sylvester the Mummy, as well as other novelties.

For a different view of the waterfront, board one of the **Argosy Cruises (p. 73)** that leave from Pier 55 for a one-hour spin around Elliott Bay.

End the day with dinner at **Brooklyn Seafood, Steak & Oyster House (p. 21).** Continuing the aquatic theme, wash down some oysters on the half shell with a dirty martini.

PIKE PLACE MARKET   SEATTLE AQUARIUM

led a successful grassroots effort to preserve it in 1971, when the market was designated a Historic District.

In a city wired on technology and caffeine, the market is a low-tech, old-world anachronism. Merchants sell goods that they make or cultivate themselves, artists live and work in studios above the shops, and street musicians have an established pecking order in designated sidewalk spots. Outdoor café seating in the bistros and pubs of Post Alley adds a European flair – although the mood can be spoiled by wall-to-wall people and near-impossible parking. Not all the vendors here have discovered the virtues and vices of plastic, so be sure to bring some cash. Visitors who put up with the bustle will enjoy an intimate experience filled with surprises.

 MAP 2 C2 ✪33 PIKE PL. AND VIRGINIA ST. BTWN. 1ST AVE. AND WESTERN AVE. 206-682-7453
HOURS: MON.-SAT. 9 A.M.-6 P.M.; SUN. 11 A.M.-5 P.M.

SEATTLE AQUARIUM

Divers say Puget Sound's icy depths produce some of the most colorful underwater wildlife in the world. Short of donning your scuba gear, the Seattle Aquarium is the best way to see it.

Seattle's first aquarium was opened in 1938 by local legend Ivar Haglund, famous for his Ivar's Acres of Clams restaurants. The exhibit's three tanks – which held fish, seals, and Oscar the Octopus – were tremendously popular. Ivar closed up shop in 1956, and an eager public waited 20 years for a new municipal facility while politicians squabbled over where to put it. Finally, the Seattle Aquarium opened in May 1977, in the center of the waterfront on Pier 59.

Visitors can marvel at 350 species of aquatic animals and plants, and resident favorites include harbor seals, sharks,

SEATTLE ART MUSEUM   WASHINGTON STATE FERRIES

giant Pacific octopuses, and sea otters that charm everyone as they float while holding hands. The aquarium's innovative programs produced the first giant octopus bred in captivity and the first exhibit-based salmon hatchery and fish ladder. The 400,000-gallon Underwater Dome is unparalleled, worthy of the trip alone: Descend into a half-sphere to find scores of deep-sea creatures completely surrounding you.

As an added treat, the adjacent IMAX Dome shows the 1980 eruption of Mount St. Helens on a 3,600-square-foot dome screen, accessible with a combined Aquarium/IMAX Dome ticket.

 MAP 2 D2 ⊕58   1483 ALASKAN WAY 206-386-4320
HOURS: MEMORIAL DAY-MID-SEPT. DAILY 10 A.M.-6 P.M.;
MID-SEPT.-MEMORIAL DAY TUES.-SUN. 10 A.M.-5 P.M.

SEATTLE ART MUSEUM

At the Seattle Art Museum (SAM), the art starts even before you walk through the doors: the 48-foot, 26,000-pound *Hammering Man* moving sculpture by Jonathan Borofsky greets visitors and passersby on the plaza outside. With expanding repositories specializing in Asian, African, coastal Native American, Greco-Roman, and modern art, the museum can't quite contain its collections and has outgrown four buildings.

SAM first opened in 1933 in Volunteer Park, at a location that is now home to the Seattle Asian Art Museum (SAAM). The museum acquired many of its early works from Richard Fuller, who used his considerable family inheritance to purchase art from collectors eager to sell during the Great Depression. SAM was already bursting at the seams when the Samuel H. Kress collection of European masters was moved to the Fine Arts Hall at Seattle Center for the 1962 World's Fair. Afterward, more room was borrowed next door at United Kingdom Hall. While in this space, SAM was one of only six American museums to host the traveling exhibit of King Tutankhamen.

A new home was built for SAM in 1991 during an ongoing revitalization of downtown. The exterior design by Robert Venturi won the International Award for Architecture in Stone in 1993, although many criticize the internal grand staircase as "a stairway to nowhere." With the construction of the new building, the organization split into two affiliated museums, with the Asian collection staying on Capitol Hill to become SAAM.

The gallery has a permanent collection of more than 23,000 works, and its reputation attracts a continuous roster of special exhibitions from around the world. And the museum is growing yet again — construction has begun for a new addition to the current location. Major construction, which may disrupt traffic, should last until 2006, with the new building opening in 2007. The Olympic Sculpture Garden, an 8.5-acre waterfront art park, is scheduled to open in 2006.

 MAP 2 D3 ✪ 60   100 UNIVERSITY ST. 206-654-3100
HOURS: TUES.-WED., FRI.-SUN. 10 A.M.-5 P.M.,
THURS. 10 A.M.-9 P.M.

WASHINGTON STATE FERRIES

They're boats...they're commuter vehicles...they're the means to an island escape. However you look at it, the ferries that traverse Elliott Bay are fixtures of the Seattle waterfront. Sightseers enjoy observing the boats make their stately way across the water as much as passengers enjoy catching city views from the ferries' decks.

For the first half of the 20th century, interisland travel was conducted by means of "Mosquito Fleet" steamer ships. The restored *Virginia V* is the only one of those to survive and was recognized in 1992 as a National Historic Landmark. The current Washington State Ferries system was formed in 1951 to usher in the modern era of marine highways. It is the largest ferry system in the United States, and its 29 boats, serving 10 routes, carried nearly 25 million passengers in 2004 alone. M/V *Wenatchee* and M/V *Tacoma* are the latest Mark II-class vessels running the Bainbridge Island route, each with a capacity of 218 vehicles and 2,500 passengers. Even so, the wait for car transport can be several hours on summer weekends. To avoid the lines, take the footbridge at 1st and Marion Streets and walk on for a nominal round-trip fare.

The Coleman Dock at Pier 52 serves as a launching point for two destinations: Bainbridge Island and Bremerton.

EXPERIENCE MUSIC
PROJECT

PACIFIC SCIENCE CENTER

Most visitors prefer the former — the trip is only 30 minutes, and the village of Winslow on the other end is an easy walk from the terminal. A dozen restaurants and a smattering of gift shops and galleries provide a pleasant way to pass the time until you catch the next boat back. Schedules are published quarterly, and they can be picked up from any hotel concierge.

From your ferry vantage point, you'll take in some of the best long-distance views of Seattle. There are occasional orca whale sightings (often, they'll make announcements of these over the ship's PA system), and when the sun shines, the Olympic Mountains come into full view.

  801 ALASKAN WAY, PIER 52 206-464-6400
HOURS: FIRST BOAT TO BAINBRIDGE ISLAND MON.-FRI.
5:30 A.M., SAT.-SUN. 6:10 A.M.; LAST BOAT TO THE
MAINLAND MON.-FRI. 12:55 A.M., SAT.-SUN. 1:25 A.M.

MAP 3 | BELLTOWN/QUEEN ANNE

EXPERIENCE MUSIC PROJECT

Love it or hate it, there is no mistaking the colorful, amorphous blob that is Experience Music Project (EMP). The Frank Gehry–designed building officially represents "the energy and fluidity of music"; local urban legend holds that it represents smashed Fender Stratocasters.

EMP is the brainchild — some say plaything — of Paul Allen, Microsoft's second-most-famous billionaire. Known to play a pretty mean guitar lick himself, Allen initially wanted a place to showcase his collection of Jimi Hendrix memorabilia. With cofounder Jody Patton on board, the scope of the project grew by the time it opened in June 2000 to celebrate nothing less than American musical innovation itself.

In theory, EMP is a museum, with a repository of 80,000 artifacts documenting the history of rock 'n' roll. In practice, it's more of a musical adventure, with interactive exhibits and live performances. The audiovisual onslaught starts at the *Roots and Branches* moving sculpture, which plays compositions from every influential music genre. Throughout the building, 75 informative videos play on plasma monitors and LED screens. Physical displays are supplemented by virtual ones in a digital collection that visitors explore on multimedia workstations. The audio orgy continues in the Sound Lab, where budding musicians generate their own 15 minutes of fame in front of a simulated audience of thousands of lighter-waving, screaming fans. And for the ultimate in interactivity, travelers journey through musical history on a 3-D amusement park–style ride.

A vast network of computer servers and enough cable to circle the globe run all this technology, and the state-of-the-art equipment comes at a price: Admission fees are high and don't include tickets for live performances in the Sky Church. But if you love rock 'n' roll, there's no place like EMP. Plus, seven days a week there is free live music at the elbow room–only Liquid Lounge.

 MAP 3 D3 ✪ 28 325 5TH AVE. N. 206-367-5483
HOURS: LABOR DAY–MEMORIAL DAY SUN., TUES.–THURS. 10 A.M.–6 P.M., FRI.–SAT. 10 A.M.–8 P.M.; MEMORIAL DAY–LABOR DAY DAILY 10 A.M.–8 P.M.

PACIFIC SCIENCE CENTER

This museum at the Seattle Center plaza is a playground for the senses. Five buildings of hands-on exhibits, two IMAX theaters, and a planetarium make science, math, and technology fun even for the non-geek.

Like the nearby Space Needle and monorail, the Pacific Science Center was built for the 1962 World's Fair, during which the pavilion served as the Federal Science Building. This graceful complex, with its trademark neo-Gothic arches, was designed by Washington State native Minoru Yamasaki, most famous as the architect of New York's original World Trade Center towers.

At the Pacific Science Center, visitors engage their senses of sight, sound, and touch in permanent exhibits highlighting creatures big and small. Unlike the stationary skeletons in a natural history museum, dinosaurs here are moving, roaring, animatronic beasts inhabiting a semitropical Mesozoic jungle. Even more real are the specimens at Insect Village, where the non-squeamish

THAT OTHER MICROSOFT GUY

Microsoft cofounder Paul Allen may not be as internationally known as former partner — and fellow billionaire — Bill Gates, but the Seattle native has definitely had much more of an impact on the city's social landscape. Not only did Allen purchase the Seattle Seahawks in 1997, but he also went on to finance the construction of Qwest Field for the team. In 2000, he founded — and funded — the **Experience Music Project (p. 8)**, which was inspired by his lifelong passion for local legend Jimi Hendrix. More recently, Allen collaborated with the likes of George Lucas, Steven Spielberg, and James Cameron to bring forth the **Science Fiction Museum and Hall of Fame (p. 64)**.

can touch live, hissing cockroaches, millipedes, walking sticks, and hairy tarantulas. The brightest spot in the museum is the Tropical Butterfly House, where hundreds of lepidoptera flutter freely about as you stroll along the garden path. It's common for a winged wonder to alight on your shoulder, purse, or hat, so everyone is checked for fluttering hitchhikers as they leave.

If that's not enough entertainment, join the more than 500,000 people who visit annually to enjoy the larger-than-life action projected on four-story screens at the Eames and Boeing IMAX theaters. The center rotates a half dozen film selections every few months, and museumgoers can save some money by getting a pass good for both the exhibits and the theaters. At night, the stars come out, with free shows in the Willard Smith Planetarium and a lineup of laser shows (for a small admission fee) featuring the music of, among others, Zeppelin, U2, and the Beatles.

 200 2ND AVE. N. 206-443-2001
HOURS: JUN.-AUG. DAILY 10 A.M.-6 P.M.; SEPT.-MAY
MON.-FRI. 10 A.M.-5 P.M., SAT.-SUN. 10 A.M.-6 P.M.

SPACE NEEDLE

With its sleek steel beams and saucer top, the Space Needle defines the Seattle skyline. Practically synonymous with the city, it is featured on the face of almost every poster, picture book, and tourist brochure of Puget Sound, often with stunning Mount Rainier as a backdrop.

Built for the 1962 World's Fair, the Space Needle became the most prominent symbol of the exhibition's 21st-century theme, presenting a bold vision of the future inspired by

SPACE NEEDLE

SEATTLE ASIAN ART MUSEUM

technology and human ingenuity. During the first six months of the fair, more than two million people flocked to the Space Needle, and today it runs neck and neck with Pike Place Market as the number-one visitor destination in town. It remains a central figure for local events as well, hosting weddings, Seattle International Film Festival parties, and New Year's Eve fireworks. The roof of the halo gets dolled up for special occasions: At one time or another, it has featured a holiday tree, a replica of the Wheel of Fortune, a giant NCAA basketball, and an inflatable baseball in honor of the Mariners' first playoff appearance.

Resident Seattleites are fond of the landmark, though many will admit to going up in it only when hosting out-of-town guests. The adult ticket fee for the 60-second elevator ride to the observation deck is $12. But once there, visitors perched 520 feet up on a clear day are treated to unsurpassed views of Mount Rainier, the Cascade and Olympic mountain ranges, downtown, and Puget Sound. Tip: If you eat at Sky City, the Needle's revolving restaurant, the ride up is free.

 D3 ✪31   400 BROAD ST. 206-905-2100
HOURS: SUN.-THURS. 9 A.M.-10 P.M.,
FRI.-SAT. 9 A.M.-MIDNIGHT

 CAPITOL HILL

SEATTLE ASIAN ART MUSEUM

In the middle of Volunteer Park on Capitol Hill is a 1933 art moderne structure flanked by two replicas of Ming Dynasty camels from the tomb of a 15th-century prince. This building, designed by architect Jay Gould, serves as the showcase for arguably the finest art in the city. Originally home to the Seattle Art Museum (SAM), it now houses the affiliated Seattle Asian Art Museum (SAAM), a world-renowned, revolving collection of art from Japan, China, Korea, India, Southeast Asia, and the Himalayas.

The city's reputation as a stronghold for Asian art and culture began with the private collection of Richard Fuller. This young art enthusiast made good use of money inherited from his father to build the museum and amass an impressive collection during the Great Depression, when everyone else was selling. Fuller's affinity for Chinese jade and ceramic snuff bottles, Japanese Buddhist sculpture, and representational works of Hindu gods and goddesses led to the establishment of a permanent collection that now numbers more than 7,000 objects.

SAAM became its own entity in 1991, yet maintains a symbiotic relationship with its downtown parent. Together, the museums have an ongoing commitment to make art accessible. Admission is by suggested donation only, and a ticket to one museum gives visitors a discount at the other. One caveat: To attract the best temporary installations, SAAM charges extra for special exhibitions. Check ahead for ticket prices.

Permanent exhibits rotate regularly to keep the full collection in circulation. The Japanese repository is among the top five in the United States, and scholars travel from all over the globe to study the Buddhist sculptures. This is one of the few places in the world where you can view rare Korean celadon and early Thai ceramics just a room away from exquisite kimonos and hanging scrolls.

 MAP 4 B4 ❼ 1400 E. PROSPECT ST. 206-654-3100
HOURS: WED.-SUN. 10 A.M.-5 P.M., THURS. 10 A.M.-9 P.M.

HARVARD-BELMONT HISTORIC DISTRICT
Railroad magnate Sam Hill lived among the Tudor and Georgian Revival mansions in this neighborhood, which is listed in the National Register of Historic Places.

 MAP 4 B2 ❹ BOUNDED BY BELLEVUE PL., BROADWAY, AND BOYLSTON AND HARVARD AVES.

LAKE VIEW CEMETERY
Old 1850s tombstones of city pioneers lie alongside the gravesites of Seattle's Bruce Lee and his son, Brandon. Glance up from your headstone-reading to take in some inspiring views.

  MAP 4 A3 ❷ 1554 15TH AVE. E.

HARVARD-BELMONT HISTORIC DISTRICT   WOODLAND PARK ZOO

MAP 5 | FREMONT/WALLINGFORD

WOODLAND PARK ZOO

Bobo, the grouchy gorilla. Nile and Potentate, the camels. Sultana, the prolific tigress (54 cubs). Geronimo, who starred with Charlton Heston in *The Pigeon That Took Rome*. These are a few of the famous residents who have drawn generations of families to the Woodland Park Zoo for more than a hundred years.

Call it animal magnetism, if you will, but herds of people have flocked to see the zoo attractions since lumber baron Guy C. Phinney opened his private menagerie for public viewing in 1877. The park gained international acclaim in the late 1970s under director David Hancocks, whose revolutionary ideas for presenting animals in their native environments led the zoo conservation movement. Visitors now experience a virtual jaunt around the world while visiting exhibits from the African Savannah to Tropical Asia, from the Northern Trail (Alaska) to the Tropical Rain Forests. Other celebrities at the zoo are Manis and Langka, two male Sumatran tiger cubs born to parents Rakata and JoJo in September 2004.

It's a trek to see all the exhibits, and it can be hard to spot, say, the leopards in their natural habitat. After exhausting the possibilities of 92 acres of 300 animal species, weary wanderers can refuel at the Rainforest Café or relax in the rose garden, with its 280 varieties of blooms.

 A2 ✪1   N. 50TH ST. AND FREMONT AVE. N. (SOUTH GATE)
206-684-4800
HOURS: MAY-MID-SEPT. DAILY 9:30 A.M.-6 P.M.;
MID-SEPT.-APR. DAILY 9:30 A.M.-4 P.M.

FARM FRESH

Thanks to Seattle's moist weather conditions, numerous produce farms flourish just outside city limits. Day trips can easily be made to Snoqualmie Valley, northeast of Seattle, where "U-Pick" fields of berries, apples, and pumpkins can be scoured at **Remlinger Farms.** Farther north, the quaint towns of La Conner and Mount Vernon overflow with lily, daffodil, and tulip patches, particularly during spring's **Skagit Valley Tulip Festival.** And although grapes are mostly grown in eastern Washington, they are aged to perfection at such wineries as the **Columbia Winery** and **Chateau Ste. Michelle** in Woodinville.

REMLINGER FARMS
32610 NE 32ND ST., CARNATION
425-333-4135
www.remlingerfarms.com

SKAGIT VALLEY TULIP FESTIVAL
100 E. MONTGOMERY ST., STE. 250, MOUNT VERNON
360-428-5959
www.tulipfestival.org

COLUMBIA WINERY
14030 NE 145TH ST., WOODINVILLE
800-488-2347
www.columbiawinery.com

CHATEAU STE. MICHELLE WINERY
14111 NE 145TH ST., WOODINVILLE
425-415-3300
www.ste-michelle.com

MAP 6 | UNIVERSITY DISTRICT

BURKE MUSEUM OF NATURAL HISTORY AND CULTURE

Tucked away on the University of Washington (UW) campus is the only major natural history museum in the Northwest. Because its curators are (understandably) more concerned with preserving artifacts than they are with public relations, many people in Seattle don't know that some of the region's largest exhibits of native arts, birds, mammals, and fossils are being displayed right in their own backyard. The museum was established by stu-

BURKE MUSEUM OF
NATURAL HISTORY
AND CULTURE

WASHINGTON PARK ARBORETUM

dents from the UW Young Naturalists' Society in 1885,
and in 1899, it became known officially as the Washington
State Museum and was relocated downtown. Back on
campus in 1964, the new Burke Museum opened after
Caroline McGilvra Burke bequeathed several million dol-
lars to the museum in honor of her late husband.

One permanent exhibit here is the kid-friendly "Life and
Times of Washington State," home to an allosaurus, a
mastodon, a sloth, and a saber-toothed tiger. Adults
might better appreciate
"Pacific Voices," the fifth-
largest restoration effort
in the world for Pacific Rim
cultures, which includes an
impressive display of rain
shields, face masks, and
native dress. Special collections are featured several times a year, and the
museum also sponsors
worldwide field research.

 A3 ✪ 12 UNIVERSITY OF
WASHINGTON, 45TH
ST. NE AND 17TH AVE.
NE 206-543-5590
HOURS: DAILY
10 A.M.-5 P.M.

WASHINGTON
PARK ARBORETUM

To walk through the arboretum is to see the forest for
the trees – all 5,500 varieties of them. Opened in 1934,
this 230-acre urban wood-
land was designed by James

SIDE WALKS

The best way to see the University District neighborhood is
to walk University Way, locally
known as "The Ave," from one
end to the other. **The University Book Store (p. 57)** is more
than just a textbook repository – you'll find countless gifts,
Husky merchandise, and unusual books, as well as a café.

Lunch at **Than Brothers (p. 32)**
will be student-priced, but the
pho won't be undergrad quality.

Across the street, **Bulldog
News (p. 56)** attracts the
worldly reader with its international assortment of newspapers and periodicals.

At the end of your route, rest
your sore feet at the **Big Time
Brewery (p. 43)** for a locally
produced microbrew or two
in a hip, collegiate (non-frat
house) setting.

F. Dawson, who worked at the famed Olmsted Brothers landscape architecture firm.

The arboretum is a living museum of 40,000 trees and shrubs grouped by species, with quaint names like Honeysuckle Hill, Azalea Way, and Loderi Valley. Three groups maintain the park and provide an outdoor class-room for education, conservation, and research: the University of Washington Center for Urban Horticulture, the Department of Parks and Recreation, and the Arboretum Foundation.

Money and manpower shortages have left the place looking a bit like a faded rose; only hints of its former beauty remain. Walking paths disappear and reemerge in the foliage, interpretive markers are hidden like Easter eggs, and the Lookout Gazebo is now a misnomer, its once-commanding view hidden in the jungle. Fortunately, a master plan to revitalize the park was unanimously approved by the city council in 2001, and fundraising activities are in full swing.

No one seems to mind the overgrowth, though, in the sol-ace and scenery of the forest canopy. The arboretum is inviting year-round – in every season, there are a half dozen species in full glory. The Graham Visitor Center, at the north entrance off Foster Island Road, is a good place to start a stroll. Or take the quintessential Sunday drive down Lake Washington Boulevard or Arboretum Drive East. Fall is not to be missed, when Japanese maples and Chilean fire trees are ablaze with color.

Make sure to save time for the Japanese Garden. These immaculate grounds are separate from the rest of the wooded wild abandon, and there's a modest $3 entry fee. It's a small price to pay to find inner peace amid the great outdoors.

 E5**26** 2300 ARBORETUM DR. E. 206-543-8800
GROUNDS HOURS: DAILY DAWN-DUSK
VISITORS CENTER HOURS: DAILY 10 A.M.-4 P.M.

UNIVERSITY OF WASHINGTON
Roam 300 acres of lush grounds to check out handsome 1895 Gothic buildings, the United States' largest medicinal herb gar-den, and the cathedral-like Suzzallo Library. Brochures are avail-able at the information office.

 C3**20** 4014 UNIVERSITY WAY NE
206-543-9198

UNIVERSITY OF WASHINGTON

HIRAM M. CHITTENDEN LOCKS

MAP 7 BALLARD

HIRAM M. CHITTENDEN LOCKS

This engineering masterpiece is a legacy of the early pioneers, who reshaped land and sea to serve the logging, mining, and fishing industries. Dedicated on July 4, 1917, the Chittenden Locks sit at the western end of the Lake Washington Ship Canal.

The locks' two navigational canals represent the culmination of the life's work of Brigadier General Hiram Martin Chittenden of the U.S. Army Corps of Engineers. Thanks to his efficient design, water pressure alone can raise or lower anything – from a one-person kayak to a 100-million-gallon oil tanker – 24 vertical feet in 15 minutes or less. During every cycle, an average of eight million gallons of water are displaced in the large channel, half a million in the small channel. The system works so well that the only significant upgrades have been to switch from cable to mechanical gates in 1966 and 1975, and to institute hydraulics in 1998.

It is fascinating to watch the process in action. Every year, 1.5 million people line the piers in all kinds of weather to mark

SIDE WALKS

The Ballard neighborhood has a rich and vibrant history and is well worth exploring beyond the locks. Save plenty of time to trawl through **Archie McPhee (p. 57)**, a store so eclectic and fun, it's nearly impossible to describe.

The rest of the **Ballard (p. 57)** shopping district is full of sweet boutiques and eclectic stores like Olivine Atelier and Lucca Great Finds.

When you get hungry, stop in **Thaiku (p. 33)**, one of the city's best Thai noodle houses.

End your Ballard tour at **Portalis (p. 44)**, a combination wine bar and wine shop with more than 30 vintages available by the glass.

the passage of 50,000 vessels for recreation, fishing, and transportation of two million tons of commercial cargo. Another highlight is watching the chinook, coho, and sockeye salmon migrate up the 21-level fish ladder to spawn. If you'd like to experience the locks firsthand by boat, Argosy Cruises offers a two-hour narrated tour, which departs from Pier 56 downtown.

 3015 NW 54TH ST. 206-783-7059
GROUNDS HOURS: DAILY 7 A.M.–9 P.M.
VISITORS CENTER HOURS:
MAY–SEPT. DAILY 10 A.M.–6 P.M.;
OCT.–APR. THURS.–MON. 10 A.M.–4 P.M.

OVERVIEW MAP

DISCOVERY PARK

As the name suggests, visitors find something new every time they explore these lush woodlands on the tip of Magnolia Peninsula. Discovery Park is a largely untamed microcosm of Pacific Northwest topography, encompassing two miles of tidal beaches, grassy meadowlands, shifting sand dunes, forested groves, and plunging sea cliffs.

The same remote location that gives Discovery Park its seclusion also makes it challenging to find. But for those who persevere, the reward is a tranquil preserve as close to what nature intended as possible. The east entrance leads to the visitors center, North Beach, and a picnic area with a bird's-eye view of Shilshole Bay Marina and Golden Gardens. Down a winding lane is the Daybreak Star Indian Cultural Center, highlighting the Duwamish people, who fished and gathered blackberries here as far back as 4,000 years before Scandinavian settlers came.

The southwest entrance is the closest to some former parade grounds, where families gather to picnic, fly kites, pick blackberries in August, and take in sweeping views of Elliott Bay and the Olympic Mountains from the promontory. Down the trail at South Beach, clam-diggers harvest mollusks in 50 yards of mud at low tide.

The park unveils more secrets to those who hike its unpaved trails. But stay inside the barriers warning explorers away from the bluffs: In 1997, entire hundred-yard sections of the hillside slid back into the sea after an especially rainy season.

OVERVIEW MAP B1 **3801 W. GOVERNMENT WAY 206-386-4236**
VISITORS CENTER HOURS:
TUES.–SUN. 8:30 A.M.–5 P.M.; PARK CLOSES AT DUSK

RESTAURANTS

Hottest restaurant of the moment: **CROW,** p. 22

Most worth-it three-figure meal: **MISTRAL,** p. 26

Best Northwest decor: **CASCADIA RESTAURANT,** p. 24

Most romantic: **ROVER'S,** p. 34

Best fine dining in Pike Place Market: **CAMPAGNE,** p. 21

Best view: **RAY'S BOATHOUSE,** p. 34

Best seafood: **FLYING FISH,** p. 25

Best after-dinner drink experience: **CHEZ SHEA,** p. 22

Best pan-Asian food: **WILD GINGER,** p. 24

Best Greek food interpretation: **LOLA,** p. 26

PRICE KEY

$ ENTRÉES UNDER $10

$$ ENTRÉES $10-20

$$$ ENTRÉES OVER $20

MAP **1** **PIONEER SQUARE/INTERNATIONAL DISTRIC**

CAFÉ PALOMA   *QUICK BITES • MEDITERRANEAN* $

Some things are more pleasing in miniature – like this tiny Pioneer Square retreat that serves pressed *panini* and freshly squeezed orange juice. While eating, enjoy the pedestrian hustle of the streets or the rotating art exhibits hung on the colorful walls.

 A2 **R** 4   93 YESLER WAY
206-405-1920

CHINA GATE   *AFTER HOURS • DIM SUM* $$

Dim sum carts are easy to find in the International District, but China Gate offers a special dumpling experience. In addition to all the pork and seafood favorites, many veggies, like eggplant and Chinese greens, get great treatment here.

 C5 **R** 37   516 7TH AVE. S.
206-624-1730

**GRAND CENTRAL BAKING
COMPANY**   *QUICK BITES • SANDWICHES* $

This old-fashioned brick building plays a big part in the Northwest's artisanal bread history. Since 1972, the Grand Central has supplied restaurants around the city with exceptional loaves and has created great sandwiches, like the basil egg salad and the focaccia with havarti and roasted vegetables, for its Pioneer Square patrons.

 B2 **R** 11   214 1ST AVE. S.
206-622-3644

MANEKI   *QUICK BITES • JAPANESE* $$

Although its origins are lost in legend, Seattle's oldest Japanese restaurant celebrated its 100th anniversary in 2004 and retains a traditional atmosphere with bilingual menus and tatami-floored back rooms. The food offerings include fresh sushi and remarkable appetizer specials, such as the tempura-fried smelt and the scallop and mushroom sautée.

 B5 **R** 28   304 6TH AVE. S.
206-622-2631

SALUMI   *HOT SPOT • DELI* $

Whenever it's open, Armandino Batali's bowling lane of a space is packed with customers clamoring for his oxtail sandwiches and house-crafted salamis. They gather around the deli's big single table and chat with tablemates, whom they know share their devotion to great meat.

 B3 **R** 23   309 3RD AVE. S.
206-621-8772

SHANGHAI GARDEN   *BUSINESS • CHINESE* $$

The decor here may need an update, but Shanghai Garden's food stands out among the many Chinese restaurants in the International District. Along with all the standards, there are also more unusual items like the wonderful black moss and bamboo fungus soup, the signature hand-shaved barley noodles, and high-nutrition fried brown rice.

 C5 **R** 36   524 6TH AVE. S.
206-625-1689

SALUMI TAKOHACHI

TAKOHACHI *QUICK BITES • JAPANESE* $

A happy octopus on Takohachi's sign beckons hungry diners inside, where they can experience Japanese comfort food – ramen, black cod *kasuzuke,* and croquettes are the favorites. Don't look for much sushi, but do enjoy the friendly atmosphere fueled by the many young Japanese expats.

 B5 **R** 30   610 S. JACKSON ST.
206-682-1828

ZEITGEIST COFFEE *CAFÉ* $

Zeitgeist is one of Seattle's classic coffeehouses. With warm woods, exposed brick, lofty ceilings, wireless Internet access, and excellent coffee, it makes a great place to relax and linger. Look for the art exhibits and film screenings, too.

 B3 **R** 26   171 S. JACKSON ST.
206-583-0497

DOWNTOWN

ALEXANDRIA'S ON SECOND *HOT SPOT • SOUTHERN* $$$

Alexandria's chef Michael Franklin turns out upscale Southern food, cooking up entrées like shrimp jambalaya and smothered pork with a side of black-eyed peas and dessert classics like sweet potato pie. The separate bar is very popular with the after-work crowd.

 B2 **R** 13   2020 2ND AVE.
206-374-3700

BROOKLYN SEAFOOD, STEAK & OYSTER HOUSE *BUSINESS • PACIFIC NORTHWEST* $$$

Highly favored among Seattle's business population, the Brooklyn is a classic steakhouse with some of the best chops in town. The oyster bar features more than a dozen varieties, and the martinis are everything you'd expect.

 D4 **R** 65   1212 2ND AVE.
206-224-7000

CAMPAGNE *ROMANTIC • FRENCH* $$$

Chef Daisley Gordon regularly dips into the bounty of the market for his French-Northwest menu, where lusty house-made charcuterie shares space with polished versions of squab and rack of lamb. The less expensive downstairs bistro Café Campagne (1600 Post Alley, 206-728-2233) is the place to handle a sudden *steak frites* craving.

MAP 2 C2 R34 86 PINE ST.
206-728-2800

CHEZ SHEA *ROMANTIC • FRENCH* $$$
Chez Shea's reputation for romance is well deserved: What could be more alluring than sharing a soufflé with a view of Elliott Bay on display through arched windows? Next door in the relaxed but slinky Shea's Lounge, the cocktails flow freely, and the kitchen's open until midnight.

MAP 2 C2 R41 94 PIKE ST., STE. 34
206-467-9990

CROW *HOT SPOT • AMERICAN* $$
Reservations at this bright space housed in a former warehouse are some of the hardest to get in Seattle. Chef-owners Craig Serbousek and Jesse Thomas present a balanced wine list and a modern comfort food menu, including a house lasagna that is a local legend.

MAP 2 E5 R79 823 5TH AVE. N.
206-283-8800

EARTH & OCEAN *BUSINESS • PACIFIC NORTHWEST* $$$
Chef Maria Hines' menu concentrates on local organic farm products and, in a twist on the turf and surf concept, is divided into "earth" and "ocean" selections. Pastry chef Sue McCown's whimsical desserts, such as the www.chocolate.com cake, have a big local following.

MAP 2 D5 R68 W HOTEL, 1112 4TH AVE.
206-264-6060

THE GEORGIAN *BUSINESS • PACIFIC NORTHWEST* $$$
The Fairmont Olympic Hotel's restaurant serves exquisite food with the hushed assurance that comes from decades of feeding dignitaries. Chef Gavin Stephenson's menu lives up to the elegant setting with Northwest classics like crisp salmon with red wine marmalade.

MAP 2 C4 R55 FAIRMONT OLYMPIC HOTEL, 411 UNIVERSITY ST.
206-621-7889

LE PICHET *AFTER HOURS • FRENCH* $$
Named for the earthenware pitchers that pour its country wines, Le Pichet warms stomachs and souls with regional French dishes. Try a roasted-to-order chicken at dinner, or while away an afternoon in the corner seat with a glass of Bandol and some chicken liver terrine.

MAP 2 B2 R19 1933 1ST AVE.
206-256-1499

THE LIBRARY BISTRO *HOT SPOT • AMERICAN* $$
The Alexis Hotel's restaurant specializes in fresh takes on American classics. Despite the bookshelves, the ambience is not hush-hush: Big lizard-skin booths and lots of appetizers make this a good spot before a football or baseball game. The adjacent Bookstore Bar shares the kitchen.

MAP 2 E4 R76 ALEXIS HOTEL, 92 MADISON ST.
206-624-3646

MATT'S IN THE MARKET *ROMANTIC • AMERICAN $$*

With owner Matt Janke making multiple daily runs to market vendors
for supplies, this tiny space overlooking the Pike Place sign and a slice
of Elliott Bay arguably serves the freshest food in Seattle. Seafood is
the standout, and the oyster po' boys on the lunch menu get raves.

 C2 **R**42   94 PIKE ST., STE. 32
206-467-7909

METROPOLITAN GRILL *HOT SPOT • STEAK $$$*

Dressed in white linen, shiny brass, and dark wood, the strutting
luxury of the Metropolitan sets the tone for its deal-making clientele.
Porterhouses and filets are the lifeblood of this famous chophouse;
the excellent wine list supplies plenty of meaty reds.

 E4 **R**78   820 2ND AVE.
206-624-3287

OCEANAIRE SEAFOOD ROOM *BUSINESS • SEAFOOD $$$*

With swooping art deco glass and wood, the Oceanaire looks like the
set for a top-flight production of *Anything Goes,* and it delivers the
same jazzy vibe. Sure, it's a chain, but the dishes treat seafood with
the respect it deserves.

 A4 **R**5   1700 7TH AVE.
206-267-2277

PAN AFRICA *QUICK BITES • AFRICAN $*

Painted in vivid oranges and yellows, this small storefront on the 1st
Avenue side of Pike Place Market serves a variety of food from all
over Africa. The ground nut stew is a sure winner on a rainy day.

 C2 **R**38   1521 1ST AVE.
206-652-2461

PLACE PIGALLE *ROMANTIC • FRENCH $$$*

Place Pigalle, hidden in a back corner of Pike Place Market has a
spectacular view of Elliott Bay and a very romantic atmosphere.
Relax and enjoy the white-tablecloth service and entrées like
Alaskan halibut and rabbit roulade. For dessert, you'll find crème
brûlée done right.

 C2 **R**45   81 PIKE ST.
206-624-1756

SAZERAC *HOT SPOT • SOUTHERN $$*

Chef Jan Birnbaum's swanky restaurant in the Hotel Monaco has a
meaty, festive menu, but he reveals his Cajun craftsmanship with
homemade details: pickled vegetables, andouille sausage, and flatbreads. Brunch shines with spicy variants on the usual eggy options.

 D4 **R**66   1101 4TH AVE.
206-624-7755

TROIANI *BUSINESS • ITALIAN $$$*

Troiani bills itself as an Italian steakhouse, so red meat predomi-
nates here. But don't miss the creative antipasti selections, such
as the basil-seared ahi tuna with Ligurian olives, or the homemade
pastas, like the porcini mushroom gnocchi. There's also live guitar
music nightly.

 D4 **R**67   1001 3RD AVE.
206-624-4060

WILD GINGER *BUSINESS • PAN-ASIAN* $$

Seattle's pan-Asian pioneer still draws throngs to its huge space, a honey-toned dining room where parties of two or 12 can be seated with ease. Try a wild boar or mountain lamb satay. For a quicker bite, sit at the mah ogany bar where you can see the chefs at work.

 C3 **®48**   1401 3RD AVE.
206-623-4450

BELLTOWN/QUEEN ANNE

AFRIKANDO *HOT SPOT • SENEGALESE* $$

West African music drifts through this warm bistro, where owner Jacques Sarr introduced Senegalese cuisine to Seattle. The sunny tones of his tomato, peanut, and mustard-onion sauces gracefully complement fresh fish, root vegetables, lamb, and couscous. Come dessert time, the mango tart is delightful.

 E2 **®41**   2904 1ST AVE.
206-374-9714

APARTMENT BISTRO *HOT SPOT • NEW AMERICAN* $$$

The Apartment Bistro is one of Seattle's hippest spots to sip a martini. With its retro setting, extensive bar, and affluent air – exuded by the well-dressed patrons – this is a see and be seen spot. The short menu often features seafood and steak.

 F3 **®62**   2226 1ST AVE.
206-956-8288

ASSAGGIO RISTORANTE *ROMANTIC • ITALIAN* $$

It seems everyone dreams of a little Italian joint to call their own, and owner Mauro Golmarvi's robust greetings help patrons make such fantasies come true. Beneath reproduced Michelangelos, diners enjoy well-tuned Italian standards like carpaccio, braised lamb shanks, and Sicilian-toned fusilli with saffron and currants.

 F4 **®72**   2010 4TH AVE.
206-441-1399

BRASA *AFTER HOURS • SPANISH* $$$

Brasa, meaning "live coals" in Portuguese, is a vibrant celebration of rural Spanish food. Chef Tamara Murphy's extensive menu includes specialties like roasted suckling pig, Cazuela clams, and braised octopus. The bar's happy hour food is famous as one of the city's best.

 F4 **®68**   2107 3RD AVE.
206-728-4220

CASCADIA RESTAURANT *BUSINESS • PACIFIC NORTHWEST* $$$

Cascadia is chef Kerry Sear's personal vision of an elegant Northwest restaurant. Rich woods and the trickling namesake fountain set the stage for meals that feature regional classics reborn. The monthly menu features entrées (like grilled halibut with a leek and onion tart or tuna with rosemary garlic fries) or prix-fixe options.

MAP 3 F3 **®59**   2328 1ST AVE.
206-448-8884

ASSAGGIO RISTORANTE   EL GAUCHO

DAHLIA LOUNGE *BUSINESS • PACIFIC NORTHWEST* $$$
Dahlia, the flagship of Tom Douglas's culinary empire, is still going strong, serving up the food that made him famous. The eclectic menu and ranges from pot stickers to such comfort classics as rotisserie roast duck and the signature coconut cream pie.

 MAP 3 F4 **R 74**   2001 4TH AVE.
206-682-4142

EL GAUCHO *HOT SPOT • AMERICAN* $$$
El Gaucho is one of Seattle's few spots for true conspicuous consumption: Big cigars, big steaks, and rich Caesar salads mixed tableside find a home here. The tables in the tiered dining room are well arranged for watching the scene, while private dining rooms offer clubby luxury for business dinners.

 MAP 3 F3 **R 49**   2505 1ST AVE.
206-728-1337

FLYING FISH *BUSINESS • SEAFOOD* $$
Christine Keff's clamorous seafood restaurant has been booming since opening in 1995; the encyclopedic selection of fish, often given a soy or curry twist, makes it a local favorite. Groups should try platters of mussels, crab, and shrimp, ordered by the pound.

 MAP 3 F3 **R 61**   2234 1ST AVE.
206-728-8595

HILLTOP ALE HOUSE *QUICK BITES • AMERICAN* $$
The HillTop Ale House has everything you could ask for in a neighborhood pub: great atmosphere, a seasonally changing selection of local microbrews, and food that is a cut above the usual. The special fish tacos and the goat cheese salad are standouts.

 MAP 3 A2 **R 6**   2129 QUEEN ANNE AVE. N.
206-285-3877

LAMPREIA *HOT SPOT • ITALIAN* $$$
Scott Carsberg, who was featured in a 2004 *New York Times* series, is one of the compass points of Seattle's culinary landscape. Lampreia's menu changes seasonally, featuring everything from luxury ingredients like tuna belly to an artful Dungeness crab with honey crisp apples.

 MAP 3 F3 **R 53**   2400 1ST AVE.
206-443-3301

MACRINA BAKERY & CAFE   SAPPHIRE KITCHEN & BAR   SHIRO'S

LOLA *HOT SPOT • GREEK-MOROCCAN* $$$

The newest member of Tom Douglas's culinary empire celebrates all things Greek, without resorting to stereotypes. Make a meal of the spreads (the barrel-aged minty feta is always a solid choice), meze plates, and kebab choices; or savor the whole fish and tagine dishes on the entrée menu.

 F4 ℝ73   2000-B 4TH AVE.
206-441-1430

MACRINA BAKERY & CAFE *BREAKFAST AND BRUNCH* $

Leslie Mackie helped shape Seattle's great crust revival with her satisfying breads. Her cafés in Belltown and Queen Anne (615 W. McGraw St., 206-283-5900) offer honest fare for breakfast and lunch: muffins, scones, quiches, soups, and sandwiches made with the bakery's daily loaves. Pack a lemon tart for the road.

 F3 ℝ52   2408 1ST AVE.
206-448-4032

MISTRAL *ROMANTIC • NEW AMERICAN* $$$

Chef William Belickis is devoted to lyric little courses – his menus are a string of food haikus. This approach was controversial when Mistral first opened, but his uncompromising attitude toward his craft earned the respect of locals. The prix-fixe menu, which emphasizes regional ingredients, changes on a daily basis.

 F4 ℝ65   113 BLANCHARD ST.
206-770-7799

OTOTO SUSHI *HOT SPOT • JAPANESE* $$

Ototo strives for Tokyo flash with its graphic white, black, and red decor – and the black-clad wait staff is no exception. The emphasis is on *nigiri* and sushi, but don't overlook the cooked entrées (such as the grilled orange teriyaki chicken and marinated black cod), which are beautifully plated.

 A2 ℝ5   7 BOSTON ST.
206-691-3838

RESTAURANT ZOË *HOT SPOT • NEW AMERICAN* $$$

Set behind a rhythmic facade of tall windows, chef-owner Scott Staples' sophisticated bistro has often been cited as one of the best

PACIFIC NORTHWEST CUISINE

Pacific Northwest cuisine took off in the restaurant scene in the 1980s, and since then, it has been whittled down to its absolute essentials. It isn't Asian fusion, though there are Asian elements to it, nor is it minimalist, in spite of the emphasis on purity. The ingredients, primarily regional, are the key – salmon, Dungeness crab, fresh asparagus, fiddlehead ferns. The treatment of the food brings out the purity of the flavors and expresses respect for the natural environment, without taking itself completely seriously. To sample some of this regional style, stop in at **Cascadia (p. 24), Flying Fish (p. 25),** or **Dahlia Lounge (p. 25).**

spots in town for his treatment of Northwest ingredients. Try the wild king salmon with fava beans.

MAP 3 F4 ℝ66   2137 2ND AVE.
206-256-2060

SAITO'S JAPANESE CAFÉ & BAR   *HOT SPOT • JAPANESE* $$
Two curving bars – one for sake, the other for sushi, with a great variety of both – shape this Belltown eatery. Saito's hot menu is ample, too, so one diner can enjoy duck soup or green tea–dusted steak, while another tucks into a plate of sashimi.

MAP 3 F4 ℝ67   2122 2ND AVE.
206-728-1333

SAPPHIRE KITCHEN & BAR   *HOT SPOT • MEDITERRANEAN* $$
High atop Queen Anne Hill, Sapphire Kitchen serves up wonderful drinks and tapas that assure its continued popularity, and the house bread is outstanding. Although the menu concentrates on Spain, the North African influence (try the red Moroccan chicken with couscous) is strong, too.

MAP 3 B2 ℝ10   1625 QUEEN ANNE AVE. N.
206-281-1931

SERAFINA   *AFTER HOURS • ITALIAN* $$
Serafina's warm ochre walls give a Tuscan atmosphere to this neighborhood haunt, which draws in locals with favorites like homemade pumpkin ravioli. The long late-night menu, paired with live jazz on the weekends, makes it a jumping spot.

MAP 3 A6 ℝ8   2043 EASTLAKE AVE. E.
206-323-0807

SHIRO'S   *BUSINESS • JAPANESE* $$
Shiro Kashiba has long been the downtown king of sushi – the hefty wait for service in his ample restaurant proves his stature. Try to sit at the bar and let the chefs guide your meal: They will steer you to the freshest choices.

MAP 3 F3 ℝ54   2401 2ND AVE.
206-443-9844

BAUHAUS BOOKS
& COFFEE

EL GRECO

KINGFISH CAFE

SKY CITY   *ROMANTIC • PACIFIC NORTHWEST* $$$

The food at Sky City doesn't quite reach the heights of the Space
Needle it occupies, but this experience is really about the view – and
on a clear night, it can't be beat. Seafood is the specialty: Try the
crab cakes with curry aioli.

 MAP 3 D3 **R** 30   SPACE NEEDLE, 400 BROAD ST.
206-905-2100

TUP TIM THAI   *QUICK BITES • THAI* $

This no-fuss restaurant is a sure bet for an inexpensive pretheater
or pre-basketball dinner. Choices tend toward standard, but well-
crafted, American-style Thai, such as multihued curries fragrant with
basil, chewy panfried noodles, and the ubiquitous pad thai.

MAP 3 D2 **R** 20   118 W. MERCER ST.
206-281-8833

WATERFRONT   *BUSINESS • SEAFOOD* $$$

With its greedy views, witty decor, and lavish portions, Waterfront
both embraces and updates the waterside restaurant tradition. The
curvy bar pulls in an upscale after-work crowd, and the shimmer-
ing water of Elliott Bay appeals to courting couples and banqueting
businesspeople alike.

MAP 3 F2 **R** 47   2801 ALASKAN WAY
206-956-9171

MAP 4   CAPITOL HILL

BAGUETTE BOX   *AFTER HOURS • SANDWICHES* $

Baguette Box is a hit with lunchers and late-night noshers alike. A
chalkboard menu lists your sandwich choices, which include the
favored drunken chicken on a crusty baguette. On the side, you can
get truffle oil fries or any of several salads.

 MAP 4 F1 **R** 24   1203 PINE ST.
206-332-0220

BAUHAUS BOOKS & COFFEE   *CAFÉ* $

Despite the avant-garde name, there is a decided coziness to this
dark-hued, bookish nook, the granddaddy of Seattle's post-Starbucks

CAFFEINE CULTURE

Grunge is dead, the dot-coms are gone, but Seattle's legacy of caffeine is a nationwide phenomenon now. And it's no wonder that Seattle has such a coffeehouse culture: There's no better time to enjoy a rich dark cup of joe than a rainy day.

The original Starbucks is located in Pike Place Market, but it doesn't have any more local ambiance here than it does in Denver. More representative of what made cafés so appealing are spots like **Zeitgeist (p. 21)**, **Bauhaus Books & Coffee (p. 28),** and Victrola Coffee & Art (411 15th Ave. E., 206-325-6520).

independent cafés. Plenty of streetside seating inside and out means that self-conscious pedestrians should either dress well or walk down another street instead.

 26 301 E. PINE ST.
206-625-1600

CRAVE *BREAKFAST AND BRUNCH • AMERICAN* $$
Crave wants to be all things — and pulls it off. Offering breakfast pastries and sandwiches, as well as candlelit dinners, this spot has a strong, almost cult-like, following. For breakfast, try the cheese blintzes, and for dinner don't miss the duck confit.

 18 1621 12TH AVE. N.
206-388-0526

EL GRECO *BREAKFAST AND BRUNCH* $$
Expect a wait for brunch at this Broadway classic, justly famous for its eggs Benedict and a rotating list of pancakes (such as pumpkin, ricotta, and oatmeal). Come dinnertime, things are calmer and more European, with plates of hummus and tzatziki, olive-laced penne, and seafood-spiked risotto.

 15 219 BROADWAY E.
206-328-4604

KINGFISH CAFE *BUSINESS • SOUTHERN* $$
Every day but Tuesday, a line of hungry patrons trails out from this upscale Southern café; drinks from the copper bar and the Coaston sisters' charming family photos provide some relief from the wait. Nearly tabletop-sized slabs of cake await those who leave room for dessert.

 11 602 19TH AVE. E.
206-320-8757

MAMOUNIA *ROMANTIC • MOROCCAN* $$
It's impossible to miss the belly dancing (featured Thurs.-Sat.), but that said, the food at Mamounia is worth a visit. The menu features two-, three-, or five-course feasts but also lets diners make their own entrée choices. Dessert includes traditional mint tea.

 29 1530 BELLEVUE AVE.
206-329-5388

MONSOON *BUSINESS • VIETNAMESE* $$$

The Banh family turns out pristine, westernized versions of Vietnamese classics in this spare, elegant bistro. The wine list takes another kind of journey: to Alsace and Austria, whose gewürztraminers and Rieslings pair beautifully with the intricate spice of the cuisine.

MAP 4 C5 **R10** 615 19TH AVE. E.
206-325-2111

OSTERIA LA SPIGA *ROMANTIC • ITALIAN* $$

This strip-mall find is the stomping ground of Seattle's expat Italians. The menu spotlights stuffed flatbreads from the owner's native Emilia Romagna, and the hand-cut pastas − tagliatelle with meat sauce, green lasagna, among others − are superb. If offered, try the pecorino plate with figs instead of dessert.

MAP 4 F2 **R38** 1401 BROADWAY
206-323-8881

TANGO *HOT SPOT • TAPAS* $$

Tango, which overlooks downtown Seattle, specializes in stylish small plates, which owner Danielle Philippa characterizes as pan-Latin. In addition to many creative seafood dishes, the menu features a wide selection of cheeses, ceviches, and no less than five types of paella.

MAP 4 F1 **R27** 1100 PIKE ST.
206-583-0382

MAP 5 | FREMONT/WALLINGFORD

ASTEROID CAFE *HOT SPOT • ITALIAN* $$

A haven for rustic Italian cuisine, funky little Asteroid Cafe offers voluminous pastas and earthy braised meats. The Tuscan-centric wine list is extensive for such a cozy spot, and owner Marlin Hathaway will gladly discuss it with you. Stop in during the day for panini and espresso.

MAP 5 B4 **R5** 1605 N. 45TH ST.
206-547-2514

BANDOLEONE *HOT SPOT • LATIN* $$$

Bandoleone is a romantic spot serving innovative cuisine. Try the roasted sweet onion stuffed with Spanish cheeses, or sample a twist on an old favorite. The happy hour menu is long and bargain priced.

MAP 5 D3 **R28** 703 N. 34TH ST.
206-329-7559

JAI THAI *QUICK BITES • THAI* $

Fremont's Thai emporium is small and cluttered, but loyal customers swear by its fresh spring rolls, peanutty satay, and curries. Rice noodles get the royal treatment here in dishes like *pad see ew* and *pad kee mao*. A new Belltown location (2132 1st Ave., 206-770-7884) has them all too.

MAP 5 D3 **R24** 3423 FREMONT AVE. N.
206-632-7060

MONSOON   ASTEROID CAFE

KABUL AFGHAN CUISINE *QUICK BITES • AFGHAN* $$
Even timid eaters will appreciate the fresh tones of Kabul's Afghan meals. This Wallingford institution's green sign is a mark of things to come: Meaty skewers are showered with herbs before cooking, dumplings are stuffed with scallions, and cilantro chutney accents many dishes.

 MAP 5 B5 ®9   2301 N. 45TH ST.
206-545-9000

ROXY'S DELI *QUICK BITES • DELI* $
Roxy's has moved around the city more than a few times, but it seems to have settled in comfortably, at last, in Fremont. Great pastrami like this is hard to come by anywhere on the left coast, and loyal customers will happily follow owner Peter Glick anywhere to get it.

 MAP 5 D2 ®13   462 N. 36TH ST.
206-632-3963

TEAHOUSE KUAN YIN *CAFÉ • TEA* $
Tea takes a secondary role to coffee in Seattle, but not at this Wallingford haunt offering dozens of expertly brewed green, oolong, black, and herbal teas. Menu descriptions like "Old Man's Eyebrows," "Sparrow Tongue," and "the Laphroaig of black teas" help (sort of) with selection.

 MAP 5 B5 ®8   1911 N. 45TH ST.
206-632-2055

35TH ST. BISTRO *HOT SPOT • FRENCH* $$
Emphasizing local organic ingredients and a casual atmosphere, 35th St. Bistro is succeeding against long odds, made in part by the fact that it replaced a neighborhood institution. Classic bistro favorites like roast chicken and Caesar salad are doing much to mollify the loyalists.

MAP 5 D3 ®25   709 N. 35TH ST.
206-547-9850

 MAP 6 UNIVERSITY DISTRICT

AGUA VERDE PADDLE CLUB & CAFE *QUICK BITES • MEXICAN* $
Paddle to or from this waterfront canteen, which rents sea kayaks just downstairs. Up in the café, margaritas flow freely, and the

THAN BROTHERS   HATTIE'S HAT

Mexican American food is playful and heavy on fruity flavors. The day kitchen serves mostly tacos and tortas (sandwiches), offering more options at night.

 MAP 6 C2 **R** 19 1303 NE BOAT ST.
206-545-8570

CAFÉ LAGO *HOT SPOT • ITALIAN* $$$
In its simple, airy space, Café Lago boasts two items that are scarce in Seattle: gauze-thin homemade pasta and a well-tended, wood-fired pizza oven. From pizza margherita to lasagna and stuffed pasta purses, a meal here guarantees uncontroversial but flawless trattoria food.

 MAP 6 E4 **R** 25 2305 24TH AVE. E.
206-329-8005

CEDARS *QUICK BITES • MIDDLE EASTERN* $
Located in an old house just off the U District's main strip, Cedars has been a student favorite for many years. The Middle Eastern menu features outstanding baba ganoush and tabbouleh, and the lunchtime pita sandwiches make a great treat.

 MAP 6 A2 **R** 8 1319 NE 43RD ST.
206-632-7708

THAN BROTHERS *QUICK BITES • VIETNAMESE* $
Vietnamese noodle soup, *pho*, is cheap and reliable at this small chain. Diners can customize their broth with an array of garnishes (lime, sprouts, basil) and condiments (hot sauce, chilis, sweet sauce). Cream puffs, a Than signature, are served even before the soup arrives.

 MAP 6 A2 **R** 10 4207 UNIVERSITY WAY NE
206-633-1735

UGLY MUG CAFE *CAFÉ* $
After tramping through the rain-sodden UW campus, students and professors look to this tweedy coffee shop to warm them up with its tasty lattes and hearty sandwiches and soups. True to its collegiate roots, Ugly Mug hosts plenty of poetry readings and open-mike revues.

 MAP 6 A2 **R** 7 1309 NE 43RD ST.
206-547-3219

UNION BAY CAFE *ROMANTIC • AMERICAN* *$$$*
A few blocks from Husky Stadium, the Union Bay Cafe turns out upscale, polished food in a dining room decorated with wood, stone, and water elements. The emphasis is on natural food, and although the meat and seafood dishes star on the menu, there are vegetarian-friendly choices as well.

 A6 ⓡ14 3515 NE 45TH ST.
206-527-8364

MAP 7 BALLARD

CAFE BESALU *CAFÉ* *$*
James Miller's handcrafted pastries make Besalu a lazy morning delight. You can tell that he takes no shortcuts when making nut twists, Danishes chock-full of fruit, and the city's greenest spinach quiche. The pastry case may be the gleaming attraction, but the coffee is excellent, too.

 ⓡ1 5909 24TH AVE. NW
206-789-1463

DANDELION *ROMANTIC • AMERICAN* *$$$*
The bright yellow walls inside this tiny – and at times noisy – space match the name. The menu is on the short side, but makes up for it by featuring local ingredients and changing weekly.

 ⓡ2 5809 24TH AVE. NW
206-706-8088

HATTIE'S HAT *HOT SPOT • SOUTHERN* *$*
The twin personalities of Ballard – marine industrial and retro-hip – are fused together in this landmark café, where Southern-leaning diner classics and pie hit the spot, morning, noon, and night. The antique bar and its big pours are legendary, especially the brunch-time Bloody Marys.

 ⓡ19 5231 BALLARD AVE. NW
206-784-0175

MARKET STREET GRILL *HOT SPOT • NEW AMERICAN* *$$*
Ballard's diners and pubs are complemented by this young bistro's blend of Asian, Mediterranean, and American classics. Nothing's startling here, but there are nice details like local razor clams in a Thai-style salad, scallops nestled in pot pie, and mashed potatoes with a buttermilk tang.

 ⓡ8 1744 NW MARKET ST.
206-789-6766

THAIKU *QUICK BITES • THAI* *$*
The beloved former Fremont noodle house has moved to Ballard, but it continues to serve some of the city's best Thai meals. Do-it-yourself salad rolls make refreshing starters, and slurpy noodles are served in duck broth, curried Chinese-style, or as pad thai.

 ⓡ10 5410 BALLARD AVE. NW
206-706-7807

CAFE FLORA *BREAKFAST AND BRUNCH • VEGETARIAN* $$
Madison Park's Cafe Flora specializes in gourmet vegetarian food. Look beyond the excellent sandwiches and pizzas for more unusual entrées like Burmese curry rolls and squash polenta. Check out the tasting menu, which pairs food with wine.

OVERVIEW MAP **D5** 2901 E. MADISON ST.
206-325-9100

CANLIS *BUSINESS • STEAK* $$$
Located in upper Queen Anne, Seattle's grandest restaurant has been pleasing refined palates since 1950. Chefs Jeff Taton and Aaron Wright combine Canlis's old-boy tradition with a passion for seasonal produce. The wine list (more than 1,000 selections) is as privileged as the clientele.

OVERVIEW MAP **C4** 2576 AURORA AVE. N.
206-283-3313

THE HARVEST VINE *ROMANTIC • BASQUE* $$
Behind his copper bar, chef Joseph Jimenez de Jimenez orchestrates a nightly tapas extravaganza packed with elaborate game morsels (wild boar), Mediterranean fish (baby monkfish, scorpion fish), and simple, salty pleasures (white anchovies, marinated olives). It's a tiny sliver of Basque country in Seattle.

OVERVIEW MAP **D5** 2701 E. MADISON ST.
206-320-9771

PALISADE *BUSINESS • SEAFOOD* $$$
Palisade basks in its unbroken marina view with a plush luau decor and hearty cuisine that's appropriately celebratory. Diners feast on large portions of seafood and steak – most famously, on the cedar-baked salmon. Brunch classics feature premium ingredients, such as prime rib and Dungeness crab.

OVERVIEW MAP **D2** 2601 W. MARINA PL.
206-285-1000

RAY'S BOATHOUSE *BUSINESS • SEAFOOD* $$$
The Olympic Mountains seem a short swim away from Seattle's most famous seafood emporium. Choose to eat on the café's open deck, with a more casual menu, or in the richly appointed main dining room. Either way, simple local treats, like slippery-sweet oysters, Dungeness crab, Oregon pinots, and Washington Rieslings, are your best bet.

OVERVIEW MAP **B2** 6049 SEAVIEW AVE. NW
206-789-3770

ROVER'S *ROMANTIC • FRENCH* $$$
Chef Thierry Rautureau has long set the standard fine dining in Seattle by serving symphonic tasting menus that incorporate every extravagance the region has to offer (Columbia River sturgeon, woodland partridge, artisanal cheese), plus some faraway luxuries. Lucky vegetarians get their own five-course menu.

OVERVIEW **D5** 2808 E. MADISON ST.
206-325-7442

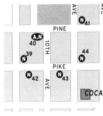 NIGHTLIFE

Hippest lounge: **BADA LOUNGE,** p. 36

Best martini selection: **TINI BIGS,** p. 39

Best beer selection: **OLD TOWN ALEHOUSE,** p. 43

Best place to see a ghost: **CHAPEL,** p. 41

Biggest dance party: **ELEMENT,** p. 38

Best drag shows: **NEIGHBOURS,** p. 42

Cheapest drinks: **CHA CHA LOUNGE,** p. 40

CATWALK CLUB *DANCE CLUB*

Less Goth than it used to be, this club still cultivates drama with nostalgic rock shows (the Misfits, the Romantics), eclectic deejayed dance nights, and the occasional fetish fashion show.

 A3 **N** 8   172 S. WASHINGTON ST.
206-622-1863

FENIX UNDERGROUND *DANCE CLUB*

Three floors of club intensity are split into two sections: The "aboveground" stages live rock and punk bands, while the "underground" features deejays spinning everything from techno to hip-hop.

 B3 **N** 15   109 S. WASHINGTON ST.
206-405-4323

MARCUS' MARTINI HEAVEN *LOUNGE*

Choose from over 75 different martini variations at this candlelit subterranean lounge, where young groups of stylish hipsters gracefully sip on very intoxicating – and very expensive – cocktails.

 A2 **N** 1   88 YESLER WAY
206-624-3323

ALIBI ROOM *BAR*

Founded as an independent filmmaker's haven, the Alibi Room houses a community library of screenplays. Little reading gets done at night, when drinks are poured and down-tempo tunes are spun.

 C2 **N** 44   85 PIKE ST., STE. 410
206-623-3180

BADA LOUNGE *LOUNGE*

It's like stepping onto a Kubrick set: whitewashed surfaces, floating video screens, and a glowing room of red floodlights. Fashionable scenesters further the decor with designer clothes – and cocktails.

A1 **N** 1   2230 1ST AVE.
206-374-8717

CONTOUR *DANCE CLUB*

Seattle's sultry after-hours mainstay, Contour keeps late-night clubbers amped all the way till 7 A.M. on weekends, with notable deejays spinning anything from house and trance to breakbeats and R&B.

F4 **N** 81   807 1ST AVE.
206-447-7704

NITELITE *BAR*

This once flashy bar has it all: country torch songs on the jukebox,

ALIBI ROOM   NITELITE

comfy booths, and generous bartenders. Cocktails are served stiff here, especially the notorious Long Island iced tea.

 B2 **N17** 1926 2ND AVE.
206-443-0899

THE PINK DOOR *BAR*

The deck at the Pink Door is a perfect spot for late-afternoon sound-gazing. After the sun goes down, enjoy live jazz and cabaret, along with free-flowing pink drinks.

 B2 **N23** 1919 POST ALLEY
206-443-3241

THE SHOWBOX *LIVE MUSIC*

Big enough for national acts, but small enough to feel like a club, The Showbox hosts many of the city's best indie rock and some hip-hop performances. Downstairs is The Green Room, an intimate piano bar.

 C3 **N46** 1426 1ST AVE.
206-628-3151

THE TRIPLE DOOR *LIVE MUSIC*

This swanky club inhabits a restored 1926 building that kept its original architectural accents. On the menu: Asian and Mediterranean. On stage: a rotating selection of pop, jazz, blues, rock, folk, and more.

 C3 **N47** 216 UNION ST.
206-838-4333

VIRGINIA INN *PUB*

Perched on a particularly charming block above the Pike Place Market, this is a conversation-friendly, smoke-free bar where you can practice your French on the first Monday of every month.

 B2 **N18** 1937 1ST AVE.
206-728-1937

ZIG ZAG CAFÉ *BAR*

Tucked into the terraced Hillclimb below the Pike Place Market, alluring Zig Zag has a Montmartre feel about it. The dark space specializes in exquisitely mixed (and exquisitely powerful) drinks.

 C2 **N43** 1501 WESTERN AVE.
206-625-1146

THE CROCODILE CAFE   CYCLOPS

MAP 3 | BELLTOWN/QUEEN ANNE

BLUWATER BISTRO *BAR*
With a spacious deck that dips into Lake Union, a signature blue margarita, and a great-looking staff, BluWater reels in a party crowd night after night.

 MAP 3 C5 N18 1001 FAIRVIEW AVE. N., STE. 1700
206-447-0769

CAFÉ VENUS AND THE MARS BAR *BAR*
Genial, tattooed service distinguishes this poppy-red café and its saloon sibling. The bar features live acts (mostly punk and honky-tonk), deejays, and a weekly moped appreciation night.

MAP 3 D6 N39 609 EASTLAKE AVE. E.
206-624-4516

CLUB MEDUSA *DANCE CLUB*
This sexy dance club is a pricey, dress-to-the-nines operation, with deejays spinning techno and trance until just before dawn on weekends. An ancient Greek theme imparts a Las Vegas feel.

MAP 3 F3 N63 2218 WESTERN AVE.
206-448-8887

THE CROCODILE CAFE *LIVE MUSIC*
There's a troublesome, sight-obscuring column in the middle of the Croc's performance space, but nobody beats the alternative rock bookings at this club co-owned by REM's Peter Buck.

 MAP 3 F3 N58 2200 2ND AVE.
206-441-5611

CYCLOPS *BAR*
Look for the single neon-blue eye to locate one of Belltown's most laid-back bars. Vinyl booths and funky artwork give Cyclops an urban edge reminiscent of Seattle '90s grunge.

 MAP 3 F3 N50 2421 1ST AVE.
206-441-1677

ELEMENT *DANCE CLUB*
Strict dress codes and exclusive VIP rooms ensure a very costly –

GUITARS AND FLANNEL

Seattle's nightlife scene gained major international attention in the early '90s when such local grunge bands as Nirvana, Pearl Jam, and Soundgarden found themselves in the global spotlight. For a slice of grunge history, check out the rockin' atmosphere – and clientele – at **Linda's Tavern (p. 41),** where Kurt Cobain used to hang out. Many of these bands got their start at the now-legendary **Crocodile Cafe (p. 38),** where even today, Eddie Vedder has been known to spontaneously jump on stage. **The Showbox (p. 37)** also served as a beginning platform for Seattle grunge bands on the rise, as well as for more recent up-and-coming local acts Modest Mouse and Death Cab for Cutie.

and very glamorous – night out at this 16,000-square-foot club, where world-class deejays spin for beautiful bodies.

 D3 **34** 332 5TH. AVE. N.
206-441-7479

GRACELAND *LIVE MUSIC*

In the heyday of grunge, the Off-Ramp provided dark sanctuary for growling vocals, ringing feedback, and driving guitars. Reborn in 1999 as Graceland, it still does.

 E6 **46** 109 EASTLAKE AVE. E.
206-381-3094

MIRABEAU ROOM *LOUNGE*

With a changing menu of featured music, the Mirabeau touches on '70s chic like a Quentin Tarantino film. Happy hour (weekdays 5-7:30 P.M.) is very happy indeed.

 D2 **22** 529 QUEEN ANNE AVE. N.
206-217-2800

RENDEZVOUS *BAR*

Once the seediest joint in Belltown, the Rendezvous was recently spiffed up. It's still a dark, unfussy place for a stiff drink and Seattle's only bar with a movie theater.

 F3 **55** 2320 2ND AVE.
206-441-5823

SHORTY'S CONEY ISLAND *PUB*

A glorious alley full of vintage video pinball machines blings and beeps in this carny-themed tavern. Despite the East Coast name, the preferred hot dog here is served Chicago style.

 F3 **57** 2222 2ND AVE.
206-441-5449

TINI BIGS *LOUNGE*

This ultra-trendy lounge may be small, but its 10-ounce signature martinis are most definitely not. The antique 1909 Brunswick bar also displays 40 hand-picked malt scotches.

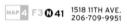 MAP 3 E2 N 40 100 DENNY WAY
206-284-0931

TULA'S RESTAURANT AND NIGHTCLUB *LIVE MUSIC*
Tula's owner, Mack Waldron, is a former navy jazz man. His no-nonsense club has given local musicians a place to jam and, frequently, to perform with touring out-of-towners.

MAP 3 F4 N 64 2214 2ND AVE.
206-443-4421

MAP 4 | CAPITOL HILL

BAD JUJU LOUNGE *LOUNGE*
Bad-ass rocker culture (flames on the walls, Megadeth in the speakers) is everywhere in this noisy, anything-goes bar, which provides comfy seats for nostalgic metalheads and poseurs alike.

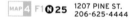 MAP 4 F3 N 41 1518 11TH AVE.
206-709-9951

THE BALTIC ROOM *DANCE CLUB*
This candlelit, lacquered club shifts personalities constantly: from mellow jazz to imported drum 'n' bass deejays to Bollywood film sets to house beats. The small dance floor emits big energy.

MAP 4 F1 N 25 1207 PINE ST.
206-625-4444

BARÇA *BAR*
A great place for a highball: sky-high ceilings, hand-painted tables, and a leopard-print chaise longue in the ladies' restroom re-create the feeling of Mediterranean paradise – with an edge.

 MAP 4 F3 N 44 1510 11TH AVE.
206-325-8263

THE CAPITOL CLUB *LOUNGE*
Vaguely Moroccan, definitely posh, the Capitol Club is a central gathering place for the Cosmopolitan-sipping set. Pierced lanterns and abundant pillows set the scene for languid lounging and flirtation.

MAP 4 F1 N 21 414 E. PINE ST.
206-325-2149

CENTURY BALLROOM *LIVE MUSIC*
With a gleaming, 2,000-foot dance floor and a stage large enough for a big big band, the Century Ballroom is a magnet for the city's best salsa and swing dancers.

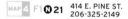 MAP 4 F3 N 40 915 E. PINE ST., 2ND FL.
206-324-7263

CHA CHA LOUNGE *BAR*
With rock 'n' roll bartenders, a Mexican wrestling/tiki theme, and

TULA'S RESTAURANT
AND NIGHTCLUB

GARAGE

killer cheap drinks, the Cha is the default bar for Seattle's writer-actor-musician types and the people who love them.

 F2 **N30** 506 E. PINE ST.
206-239-1101

CHAPEL *LOUNGE*

A refurbished funeral home, Chapel fashionably mixes its Gothic past with the cosmopolitan chic of Seattle's future. Lavender martinis and other gorgeous pours color-coordinate with the stylish crowd.

 F1 **N20** 1600 MELROSE AVE.
206-447-4180

CHOP SUEY *LIVE MUSIC*

This stylish nightspot offers an eclectic lineup that spans deejays spinning vinyl, indie rock, and hip-hop with breakdancers. The striking decor features Chinese lanterns, Bruce Lee portraits, and soft red lighting.

 F3 **N46** 1325 E. MADISON ST.
206-324-8000

GARAGE *POOL HALL*

This pool hall winks at its repair-shop past with chrome, vinyl, and a gas tank or two. It boasts 18 regulation tables and plenty of room to set up shots.

 B2 **N6** 1130 BROADWAY AVE. E.
206-322-2296

LINDA'S TAVERN *BAR*

The Montana ranch motif that marked this grunge mainstay when it opened a decade ago has faded, leaving a big, noisy bar with a great jukebox and a heated patio.

 F2 **N32** 707 E. PINE ST.
206-325-1220

MANRAY *QUEER*

Although mostly a gay men's bar, Manray, with its milky white, space-age decor, beckons anyone in search of a futuristic nightlife experience. Monitors spread out like wallpaper, playing music videos and the occasional sitcom.

 F2 **N31** 514 E. PINE ST.
206-568-0750

NEUMOS

BLUE MOON TAVERN

NEIGHBOURS *QUEER*
Seattle's biggest – and oldest – gay disco has become increasingly straight-friendly over the years. Still, packs of sweaty men dominate the space, and occasional drag shows dominate the stage.

 F2 39 1509 BROADWAY
206-324-5358

NEUMOS *LIVE MUSIC*
This hot Capitol Hill rock club opened on Valentine's Day 2004 and is now the largest venue in the neighborhood for indie and main-stream acts like The Streets and Neko Case.

 F3 N42 4925 E. PIKE ST.
206-709-9467

THE WILDROSE *QUEER*
The only lesbian bar in town, the Rose is a fixture for women looking for love or just a round of pool. It's mellow on weeknights; weekends can get steamy.

 F3 N43 1021 E. PIKE ST.
206-324-9210

MAP 5 FREMONT/WALLINGFORD

BESO DEL SOL *DANCE CLUB*
Colorful decor, plentiful margaritas, and lively bands make this neighborhood Southwestern restaurant a most welcoming place for beginners and experts to practice salsa moves. Dinner earns a danc-ing discount.

 B4 4 4468 STONE WAY N.
206-547-8087

FABULOUS BUCKAROO TAVERN *BAR*
Finding the Buckaroo is easy: Just look for neon and a string of parked motorcycles. The smallish space can get boisterous, but the Buck is still a friendly neighborhood bar.

 C3 N11 4201 FREMONT AVE. N.
206-634-3161

THE GEORGE & DRAGON PUB *PUB*

With its handsome horseshoe bar and live satellite feed, G&D gives sustenance to Seattle's Anglophiles, particularly its football (soccer) fans. Further competition is offered with Tuesday trivia nights.

 D2 12 206 N. 36TH ST.
206-545-6864

TOST *BAR*

Fremont finally got its own futuristic bar, but it's somewhat less decadent (no smoking singer-songwriters at the mike) than its Capitol Hill counterparts. The laid-back vibe fits this area perfectly.

 D2 15 513 N. 36TH ST.
206-547-0240

TRIANGLE LOUNGE *LOUNGE*

Indeed triangular, the Lounge offers a comfortable after-work watering hole in the heart of Fremont. The whole building is tagged with neon, including a "Prescriptions" sign above the bar.

 D2 17 3507 FREMONT PL. N.
206-632-0880

MAP 6 | UNIVERSITY DISTRICT

BIG TIME BREWERY & ALEHOUSE *BAR*

Mellow Big Time avoids the frat-house feel of many other U District nightspots. Choose from a spectrum of brews − from blondes to stouts − poured at a classy antique bar.

 B2 15 4133 UNIVERSITY WAY NE
206-545-4509

BLUE MOON TAVERN *BAR*

Known midcentury as a poets' haunt − Theodore Roethke and Richard Hugo were regulars − the Blue Moon still pours Northwest brews in the name of all things literary.

 A1 1 712 NE 45TH ST.
206-675-9116

TOMMY'S NIGHTCLUB *BAR*

Equal parts club and sports bar, Tommy's reels in fresh-faced UW students looking to party away their midterms at night and watch Husky games with a beer during the day.

 A2 2 4552 UNIVERSITY WAY NE
206-634-3144

MAP 7 | BALLARD

OLD TOWN ALEHOUSE *PUB*

Hardwood floors and vaulted ceilings open up this charming Old

Ballard relic, where the list of Washington State brews is extensive, and the pub fare is tasty – and reasonable.

MAP 7 N18 5233 BALLARD AVE. NW
206-782-8323

THE PEOPLE'S PUB *PUB*

German beer and pub grub (served until 1:30 A.M.) keep customers fueled at this pretense-free neighborhood bar.

MAP 7 N12 5429 BALLARD AVE. NW
206-783-6521

PORTALIS *BAR*

Adorned in vintage signs and surrounded by brick walls, this rustic wine bar/shop sells over 400 bottles from around the world, about 30 of which are available by the glass at any given time.

MAP 7 N17 5310 BALLARD AVE. NW
206-783-2007

SUNSET TAVERN *BAR*

Simultaneously hip and grungy, the Sunset is, among many things, home to Ballard's most intimate live stage and the occasional "Rockaraoke," where amateurs sing their favorites in front of a live band.

MAP 7 N11 5433 BALLARD AVE. NW
206-784-4880

TRACTOR TAVERN *LIVE MUSIC*

The unvarnished Tractor is the performing heart of Ballard's nightlife. Shows tend toward alt-country and other kinds of music filled with worldly nostalgia. Vintage Western wear is always appropriate.

MAP 7 N13 5213 BALLARD AVE. NW
206-789-3599

SHOPS

Best place to splurge: **PACIFIC PLACE,** p. 49

Best record shop: **SONIC BOOM RECORDS,** p. 55

Best shoes: **PED,** p. 49

Quirkiest tchotchke store: **DELUXE JUNK,** p. 54

Best women's clothing: **OLIVINE ATELIER,** p. 58

Best pottery shop: **LAGUNA VINTAGE POTTERY,** p. 46

Best place to feel like you're in Japan: **UWAJIMAYA,** p. 46

Most original souvenirs: **FIREWORKS GALLERY,** p. 46

Best treasure trove: **RHINESTONE ROSIE,** p. 52

Best store for free-spirited travelers:
WIDE WORLD BOOKS & MAPS, p. 56

MAP 1 PIONEER SQUARE/INTERNATIONAL DISTRICT

BUD'S JAZZ RECORDS *MUSIC*

Keeping the beat for jazz aficionados since 1982, this subterranean shop stocks thousands of vinyl records and CDs, including hard-to-find releases, by all the jazz greats. Ask Bud or James for recommendations.

MAP 1 B3 **S** 20   102 S. JACKSON ST.
206-628-0445

ELLIOTT BAY BOOK COMPANY *BOOKS*

Tomes are stacked from floor to ceiling here, filling multiple rooms in one of Seattle's most beloved bookstores. An impressive schedule offers appearances by nationally and locally acclaimed authors.

MAP 1 B3 **S** 17   101 S. MAIN ST.
206-624-6600

FIREWORKS GALLERY *GIFT AND HOME*

Gift-buying in this colorful shop is never a chore. Whimsical, functional, and always artful, many items, including glassware, pottery, jewelry, and beautifully crafted Judaica, are made by Northwest artists.

MAP 1 B2 **S** 10   210 1ST AVE. S.
206-682-9697

KINOKUNIYA BOOK STORE *BOOKS AND MUSIC*

This expansive bookstore, adjacent to the Uwajimaya Asian food empire, sells a wealth of books and magazines in Japanese, Chinese, and English – and has a top-notch Asian cookbook section.

MAP 1 C4 **S** 35   525 S. WELLER ST.
206-587-2477

LAGUNA VINTAGE POTTERY *VINTAGE*

Colorful pottery entices passersby into this turn-of-the-20th-century brick building filled with hundreds of pieces, and dozens of patterns, of vintage American pottery and dinnerware. Available by the set or piece.

MAP 1 A3 **S** 7   116 S. WASHINGTON ST.
206-682-6162

TSUE CHONG CO. *GOURMET GOODIES*

At this no-frills fortune cookie outlet, you can buy fresh noodles, crispy fortune cookies, and unfolded, unstuffed "unfortunates." Or order a customized batch stuffed with personalized prophecies.

MAP 1 C6 **S** 38   801 S. KING ST.
206-623-0801

UWAJIMAYA *GOURMET GOODIES*

Covering more than 50,000 square feet is an amazing array of Asian food from lotus roots to sushi, including an outstanding fish department, an entire aisle of rice crackers, and gifts.

MAP 1 C4 **S** 34   600 5TH AVE. S.
206-624-6248

BUD'S JAZZ
RECORDS

FIREWORKS GALLERY

LAGUNA VINTAGE
POTTERY

MAP 2 DOWNTOWN

ALHAMBRA *CLOTHING AND SHOES*
At this gracious, upscale boutique, patrons sip tea while browsing among handbags, shoes, locally made hats, silver jewelry with
semi-precious stones, and items by such designers as Trina Turk and
Burning Torch.

 MAP 2 C2 Ⓢ36 101 PINE ST.
206-621-9571

BORDERS BOOKS AND MUSIC *BOOKS AND MUSIC*
Conveniently located downtown for lunchtime browsing, this size-
able store has a comprehensive collection of books, an impressive
Northwest section, and a wide variety of CDs.

 MAP 2 B3 Ⓢ28 1501 4TH AVE.
206-622-4599

FINI *ACCESSORIES*
Perfect accessories from this pretty little store will perk up anyone's
outfit. You'll find Lulu Guinness bags, sparkly jewelry, velvety gloves,
hats, belts, and other fashionable wardrobe enhancers.

 MAP 2 C2 Ⓢ34 86 PINE ST.
206-443-0563

FLORA AND HENRI *KIDS STUFF*
You won't find cartoon characters emblazoned on tacky T-shirts
here – just sophisticated couture for the discerning child. These classic clothes with exquisite detailing have prices to match.

 MAP 2 A4 Ⓢ7 717 PINE ST.
206-749-9698

FOX'S GEM SHOP *JEWELRY*
Fox's has adorned upper-crust Seattleites and brides in dia-
monds, rings, and magnificent watches since 1912, but the jewelry is never stodgy. Classic, contemporary, and custom designs
all make a showing.

 MAP 2 C4 Ⓢ52 1341 5TH AVE.
206-623-2528

ISADORA'S ANTIQUES *VINTAGE*

This stately shop takes vintage wear to the next level. Exquisite evening gowns, suits, wedding dresses, jewelry, and accessories are in pristine condition, rightly reflected in the prices.

 B2 **$21** 1915 1ST AVE.
206-441-7711

JERI RICE *CLOTHING*

Within the elegant confines of this label lover's paradise, designer clothing from the likes of Akris and Dusan awaits women with full wallets (or unlimited credit).

 C4 **$54** 421 UNIVERSITY ST.
206-624-4000

J. GILBERT FOOTWEAR *CLOTHING AND SHOES*

Despite the name, this upscale shoe store also carries a fine selection of European clothing. Shoe fetishists will find tony styles by Taryn Rose and Paul Green.

 B2 **$15** 2025 1ST AVE.
206-441-1182

LEFT BANK BOOKS COLLECTIVE *BOOKS*

This collectively owned bookstore with leftist leanings is proud of its accumulation of non-mainstream titles. Well-stocked sections in the cramped store include "Anarchism" and "Alternative Living."

 C2 **$40** 92 PIKE ST.
206-622-0195

M COY BOOKS *BOOKS*

This small bookstore seems miles away from the city's bustle, but it's just one block up from lively Pike Place Market. It focuses on contemporary literature, art, photography, and graphic and interior design.

 C2 **$37** 117 PINE ST.
206-623-5354

METSKER MAPS OF SEATTLE *BOOKS*

Geography buffs and travelers could get lost in the comprehensive collection of celestial maps, globes, map software, topographic hiking maps, and travel books. For help, just ask for directions.

 C2 **$39** 1511 1ST AVE.
206-623-8747

NORDSTROM *CLOTHING AND SHOES*

What started as a Seattle shoe store in 1901 is now a leading retailer known for its selection of shoes and legendary service. The flagship store is worth a visit.

 A4 **$2** 500 PINE ST.
206-628-2111

OPUS 204 *CLOTHING*

Opus 204 delivers Euro flair without Euro prices. You'll find original pants, skirts, tops, and jackets by the shop's own clothing line. But you won't find yourself coming and going in similar fashions.

MAP2 B2 **$16** 2004 1ST AVE.
206-728-7707

JERI RICE   METSKER MAPS OF SEATTLE

PACIFIC PLACE *SHOPPING CENTER*
The crown jewel of downtown shopping has tenants such as Cartier, Tiffany & Co., and Williams-Sonoma. It's also known for reasonable parking fees, restaurants, and an 11-screen cinema.

MAP 2 A4 **$4** 600 PINE ST.
206-405-2655

PARFUMERIE ELIZABETH GEORGE *BATH, BEAUTY, AND SPA*
Tucked away in a downtown building is a tiny, charming perfumery run by Elizabeth George. She carries hard-to-find scents, but can also create a custom-blended fragrance just for you.

MAP 2 C4 **$50** 1424 4TH AVE.
206-622-7212

PED *SHOES*
The high-quality men's and women's shoes at this warm, intimate boutique are sure to stand out in a crowd. Don't miss the hand-crafted Cydwoq shoes, small leather goods, handbags, and locally designed jewelry.

MAP 2 E3 **$74** 1115 1ST AVE.
206-292-1767

PIKE PLACE MARKET
See SIGHTS, p. 4.

MAP 2 B2 **$33** PIKE PL. AND VIRGINIA ST. BTWN. 1ST AVE. AND WESTERN AVE.
206-682-7453

SWAY & CAKE *CLOTHING*
This favorite Seattle boutique is chock full of stuff from Rebecca Taylor, Materia Prima, and Corey Lynn Calter. Owner Tamara Donaghy-Bates carries the latest from designers. Bring a bucket of money – this shop is not cheap.

MAP 2 B4 **$29** 1631 6TH AVE.
206-624-2699

TULIP *CLOTHING*
The uncluttered atmosphere of this boutique makes it clear that clothes are the focus: Young designer labels such as Mayle, Paul & Joe, and Lauren Moffatt come in flirty styles, with a few accessories to pull your look together.

MAP 2 D3 **$63** 1201 1ST AVE.
206-223-1790

LOCAL DESIGNERS

Who says Seattle doesn't have style? The city has tons — and the local designers to prove it. Whether it's handbags, jewelry, pottery, hats, shoes, or even wedding dresses, Seattle can offer up a designer for every desire. Check out a few of these local gems. Luly Yang (1218 4th Ave., 206-623-8200) has impeccable eveningwear and bridal gowns; Barbara Dunshee designs amazing pottery, which is available at Phoenix Rising Gallery (2030 Western Ave., 206-728-2332). Missy Morrisey (206-321-8900) will even come to you: She makes house calls for custom-designed shoes.

TWIST *ACCESSORIES AND JEWELRY*
Everything here is alive with color and artfully designed — glass vases, whimsical metal sculptures, ceramics, tableware, and case upon case of arresting jewelry by internationally known designers like Cathy Waterman and Gabrielle Sanchez.

 MAP 2 A4 **$3**   600 PINE ST.
206-315-8080

UMMELINA *BATH, BEAUTY, AND SPA*
Ummelina has created "journeys" to "foreign lands" where individuals (and couples) in theme-decorated rooms receive treatment based on body rituals from around the world. Book ahead at this popular spa.

MAP 2 B3 **$27**   1525 4TH AVE., 2ND FL.
206-624-1370

WHITE HORSE *BOOKS*
The focus here is on antiquated English literature, but the wood-and-leather space with equestrian decor also doubles as a cozy English pub. Owner Joe Gilmartin serves a small wine selection and his very own White Horse ale.

 MAP 2 B2 **$24**   1908 POST ALLEY
206-441-7767

YE OLDE CURIOSITY SHOP *GIFT AND HOME*
This musty, odd shop has carried unusual items for more than 100 years. Among its treasures are Sylvester the mummy, shrunken heads, Native American art, Mount St. Helens' ash, and novelties.

 MAP 2 E3 **$75**   1001 ALASKAN WAY/PIER 54
206-682-5844

ZEBRACLUB *CLOTHING*
Think wearable art for the young and hip, and you'll be right at home when entering Zebraclub. Denim is the shop's true calling, from faded out to darker than dark.

 MAP 2 B2 **$22**   1901 1ST AVE.
206-448-7452

UMMELINA   CHARTREUSE INTERNATIONAL

MAP 3 BELLTOWN/QUEEN ANNE

CHARTREUSE INTERNATIONAL *GIFT AND HOME*
Herman Miller would feel at home among the mid-20th-century furniture in this small, mod shop. Alessi home accessories, littala glassware, and cool barware round out the goods for design aficionados.

MAP 3 F3 $48   2609 1ST AVE.
206-328-4844

LA FEMME *CLOTHING*
Only the sophisticated may apply. Blouses, suits, dresses, and sweaters from top coast-to-coast designers dot this Queen Anne gem. And it's here that you can find Frost French, Jude Law's ex-wife Sadie Frost's line.

MAP 3 B2 $11   1622 QUEEN ANNE AVE. N.
206-285-2443

QUEEN ANNE *SHOPPING DISTRICT*
This hilly and always bustling neighborhood is an eclectic blend of hip clubs, tony boutiques, beautiful parks, and great breakfast spots and cafés. For women's apparel, stop in at La Femme and the unusual but fun Queen Anne Mail & Dispatch.

MAP 3 B2 $12   QUEEN ANNE AVE. N. BTWN. ROY AND MCGRAW STS.

QUEEN ANNE BOOKS *BOOKS*
A bit on the small side, this family-oriented neighborhood bookstore carries a smattering of everything and a wide collection of children's books. The friendly staff is quick to help.

MAP 3 B2 $9   1811 QUEEN ANNE AVE. N.
206-283-5624

QUEEN ANNE MAIL & DISPATCH *CLOTHING*
This unusual establishment has a split personality: One half is a mailing service, and the other is a modern-day general store stocked with gifts, Cosabella lingerie, and trendy women's clothing.

MAP 3 A2 $4   2212 QUEEN ANNE AVE. N.
206-286-1024

LIPSTICK TRACES   RED LIGHT

RHINESTONE ROSIE *VINTAGE*
This unassuming shop is a treasure trove of sparkly vintage jewelry. Owner Rosie Sayyah, a master of rhinestone jewelry repair, can replace faux gems or convert clip earrings to pierced.

 A1 S1 606 W. CROCKETT ST.
206-283-4605

A SALON DAY SPA BOUTIQUE *BATH, BEAUTY, AND SPA*
This establishment does double duty: A spa in back offers a full range of treatments from head to toe, and the boutique up front carries understated designer clothing.

 A2 S3 2203 QUEEN ANNE AVE. N.
206-284-9200

THE TEACUP *GOURMET GOODIES*
In a town of caffeine fiends, this little shop fills the niche for tea lovers with more than 100 varieties. To brew your selection, choose from English, Japanese, and Chinese tea ware.

 A2 S2 2207 QUEEN ANNE AVE. N.
206-283-5931

MAP 4 CAPITOL HILL

BAILEY/COY BOOKS *BOOKS*
Literary and diverse, this Seattle institution in the heart of Capitol Hill caters to a nonconformist population with gay and lesbian literature, women's studies, poetry, philosophy, and thoughtfully selected fiction.

 D2 S13 414 BROADWAY AVE. E.
206-323-8842

CAPITOL HILL *SHOPPING DISTRICT*
One of the more anything-goes areas in the city, with tons of vintage shops, music stores, and cool cafés for people-watching. From mohawks to layered-bob types, there's a store for every style.

 F1 S28 E. PIKE ST. BTWN. MINOR ST. AND 14TH AVE.; BROADWAY
AVE. E. BTWN. DENNY AND ROY STS.; E. PINE ST. BTWN.
MELROSE AND 11TH AVES.

MADISON PARK

Centered along East Madison Street between 41st and 43rd Avenues (Overview Map D6), this charming shopping district is dotted with quaint ivy-covered storefronts and breathtaking views of Lake Washington and the Cascades. You could easily spend a half-day in Madison Park, which takes its name from the beautiful park that anchors this area.

Begin your shopping excursion with a massage at Spa Del Lago (1929 43rd Ave. E., Ste. 100, 206-322-5246), followed with lunch at Cactus (4220 E. Madison St., 206-324-4140) for Southwestern cuisine. And whether you want an adjustable measuring scoop from Cookin (4224 E. Madison St., 206-328-2665), baby pajamas from the Original Children's Shop (4114 E. Madison St., 206-328-7121), or conservative clothing from Yankee Peddler (4218 E. Madison St., 206-324-4218), this is where the small town shopper can find solace in the big city. For an extra dose of that Main Street, U.S.A. feeling, don't miss Bert's Red Apple Market (1801 41st Ave. E., 206-322-1330).

EDIE'S *CLOTHING AND SHOES*
Owner Erin Dolan gives each shoe its due, displaying everything prominently in Spartan surroundings. Edgy urban brands include Camper, Diesel, and Asics; choose also from hip handbags and jewelry.

 319 E. PINE ST.
206-839-1111

LIPSTICK TRACES *ACCESSORIES*
Hip chicks come here for quirky and inexpensive indulgences. The edgy, red-and-black decor of the shop serves as a backdrop for one-of-a-kind vinyl handbags, one-off body products, and clothes.

 303 E. PINE ST.
206-329-2813

RED LIGHT *VINTAGE*
This funky and fabulous vintage shop has two floors of clothing and accessories for dress-up, with everything from cat's-eye glasses to disco dresses. Check out the decorated dressing rooms.

 312 BROADWAY AVE. E.
206-329-2200

REI *CLOTHING AND SHOES*
Designed in mountain-lodge style, complete with a rushing stream, REI's flagship store is loaded with outdoor gear and clothing. It also boasts a 65-foot indoor climbing pinnacle.

 222 YALE AVE. N.
206-223-1944

MAP 5 FREMONT/WALLINGFORD

BITTERS CO. *GIFT AND HOME*

Two sisters travel the world and fill their store with finely crafted items, such as totes made from banana fibers, furniture incorporating found objects, Portuguese blankets, and jewelry.

 MAP 5 D2 **S**16   513 N. 36TH ST.
206-632-0886

BURNT SUGAR *ACCESSORIES*

One part vintage shop, one part girl haven, this colorful store carries jewelry, kitschy vintage lamps, bath products, cosmetics galore, and anything-but-boring paper products and greeting cards.

 MAP 5 D2 **S**18   601 N. 35TH ST.
206-545-0699

DANDELION BOTANICAL COMPANY *BATH, BEAUTY, AND SPA*

Refreshing natural scents fill the air of this earthy, dim apothecary, where granola types go for pure oils, handmade soaps, and the staff's expert assistance.

 MAP 5 D3 **S**29   708 N. 34TH ST.
206-545-8892

DELUXE JUNK *VINTAGE*

This former funeral parlor now gives new life to everything from outlandish lamps to retro bar sets. True junk connoisseurs will delight over aqua-colored princess phones and chrome dinette sets.

 MAP 5 D3 **S**21   3518 FREMONT PL. N.
206-634-2733

ENEXILE *CLOTHING AND SHOES*

Artsy types shop at this eclectic boutique filled with designer clothing, original artwork, furniture, rhinestone jewelry, beauty products, and posh pillows. Dogma, the store's label for clothing and accessories, is decidedly vintage.

 MAP 5 D3 **S**22   611 N. 35TH ST.
206-633-5771

ESSENZA *BATH, BEAUTY, AND SPA*

Visiting this airy apothecary is a sensual experience – splash on European fragrances, touch up your makeup, or try on silky pajamas. Don't miss the petite couture for babies.

 MAP 5 D3 **S**23   615 N. 35TH ST.
206-547-4895

FREMONT *SHOPPING DISTRICT*

With its independent, arty, and eclectic shops, Fremont is one of the best areas to spend money and just hang out for the day. Afterward, you'll have a good sense of what Seattle is all about.

 MAP 5 D3 **S**20   BTWN. EVANSTON AVE. N. AND FREMONT AVE. N., N. 34TH
AND N. 36TH AVES.

GASWORKS PARK KITE SHOP *KIDS STUFF*

A canopy of kites suspended from the ceiling radiates a rainbow of

LOLA POP   WALLINGFORD CENTER

colors; aerial navigators can choose from the basics or more deluxe
models. Toys and games are also available.

 E4 **S31** 3420 STONE WAY N.
206-633-4780

LES AMIS *CLOTHING*

Pretty, feminine clothing by such designers as Trina Turk and Nanette
Lepore grace the racks of this romantic boutique favored by locals.
There's also charming jewelry, lingerie, candles, and fragrances.

 D2 **S19** 3420 EVANSTON AVE. N.
206-632-2877

LOLA POP *CLOTHING AND SHOES*

French owner Muriel Monteiro stocks her mint-and-red boutique with
pricey *Sex and the City*-style shoes from Europe. You'll also find a
selection of clothing, chic handbags, and jewelry.

 D3 **S26** 711 N. 35TH ST.
206-547-2071

OPEN BOOKS: A POEM EMPORIUM *BOOKS*

A refuge from the mega-bookstores, this independent shop dedicated to poetry stocks new, used, and out-of-print books. Ask for the
schedule of readings by local and national poets.

 B6 **S10** 2414 N. 45TH ST.
206-633-0811

SONIC BOOM RECORDS *MUSIC*

Owners Jason Hughes and Nabil Ayers has turned this once small
indie record shop into a booming mini-chain of three incredible
record stores. It's where those who know music go. The Fremont
Avenue location has a complete vinyl shop the under main store.

 D3 **S27** 3414 FREMONT AVE. N.
206-547-2666

WALLINGFORD CENTER *SHOPPING CENTER*

This former schoolhouse (circa 1876) is now a charming venue for
more than 20 shops, among them home accessories shop Zanadia,
Crackerjack Contemporary Crafts, and Yazdi's ethnically influenced
women's clothing.

 B5 **S7** 1815 N. 45TH ST.
206-517-7773

WIDE WORLD BOOKS & MAPS *BOOKS*

The well-traveled and enthusiastic staff of this Wallingford institution is happy to provide direction in finding travel books, gear, maps,
globes, and luggage. Staff members also offer sage travel tips.

 MAP 5 B5 ❺ 6   4411 WALLINGFORD AVE. N.
206-634-3453

MAP 6 | UNIVERSITY DISTRICT

BARNES & NOBLE *BOOKS*

This mega-bookstore attracts a large contingent of students from
the nearby university, but with thousands of titles, it's a literary
feast for everyone. The ubiquitous Starbucks café is upstairs.

 MAP 6 A4 ❺ 13   2675 NE UNIVERSITY VILLAGE
206-517-4107

BULLDOG NEWS *BOOKS*

Belly up to the espresso bar with your magazine in the open-minded
atmosphere of this popular college crowd hangout. Every genre of
periodical is represented, as are foreign-language publications.

MAP 6 A2 ❺ 11   4208 NE UNIVERSITY WAY
206-632-6397

FRAN'S CHOCOLATES *GOURMET GOODIES*

This chocolatier, more boutique than candy store, is nationally
known for making luscious *gianduja* that rival any Belgian chocolate.
Confections are elegantly displayed alongside Fran's desserts and
phenomenal ice cream.

MAP 6 A4 ❺ 13   2626 NE UNIVERSITY VILLAGE
206-528-9969

MERCER *CLOTHING*

A stark interior is the first clue that you'll be paying a bit more for
the average pair of jeans. But with designers like Chip and Pepper,
Citizens of Humanity, and Blue Cult, you'll realize it's not so average,
is it?

MAP 6 A4 ❺ 13   2670 NE UNIVERSITY VILLAGE
206-388-0329

SEATTLE CAVIAR COMPANY *GOURMET GOODIES*

This swanky shop offers highbrow tastes (and tastings) without the
attitude. Cases are filled with Beluga caviar, foie gras, and truffles.
Call ahead and use the drive-up window (really).

 MAP 6 D1 ❺ 21   2922 EASTLAKE AVE. E.
206-323-3005

THE SOAP BOX *BATH, BEAUTY, AND SPA*

There are enough scents, soaps, and lotions here to keep a small
country clean. The store will even mix the fragrance of your choice
into oil, lotion, or bubble bath.

 MAP 6 A2 ❺ 5   4340 NE UNIVERSITY WAY
206-634-2379

THE SOAP BOX

BULLDOG NEWS

UNIVERSITY BOOK STORE *BOOKS AND MUSIC*
This independent college bookstore (the largest in the country) has fed the minds of students and the general public for more than a century. Check the schedule for author appearances.

 A2 **$**4 4326 NE UNIVERSITY WAY
206-634-3400

UNIVERSITY VILLAGE *SHOPPING CENTER*
Pedestrian-friendly, with upscale shops, chain stores, and independent boutiques, this open-air shopping mecca really is more village than mall. Outdoor seating, restaurants, and cafés invite shoppers to linger.

 A4 **$**13 4500 25TH AVE. NE
206-523-0622

MAP 7 | BALLARD

ARCHIE MCPHEE *GIFT AND HOME*
Rubber chickens, gag gifts, hula-girl clocks, costumes, and religious curios fill bins and shelves in this warehouse-like store devoted to playful oddities.

 $5 2428 NW MARKET ST.
206-297-0240

BALLARD *SHOPPING DISTRICT*
Some have called this area – a former fishing village – the Brooklyn of Seattle. Most go for the girlie boutiques, excellent music scene, and hip, happening pubs.

 $9 NW MARKET ST. BTWN. 15TH AND BALLARD AVES. NW; BALLARD
AVE. NW BTWN. NW MARKET ST. AND 20TH AVE. NW

CAMELION DESIGN *GIFT AND HOME*
New homebuyers or anyone looking to redecorate should check this place out for ideas, or actual furniture, for your new pad. Even an old pad could benefit from the plush, cool home stuff found here.

 $16 5330 BALLARD AVE. NW
206-783-7125

HABITUDE AT THE LOCKS *BATH, BEAUTY, AND SPA*

The woodsy environment of this lodge-like spa pays homage to the Northwest with soothing treatments such as hot rock saunas, "rain forest showers," and "togetherness massages" in the Gathering Grove.

 S4 2801 NW MARKET ST.
206-782-2898

LUCCA GREAT FINDS *GIFT AND HOME*

European antiques, exotic mounted insects, body lotions, and other unusual objects fill the nooks and crannies of this intimate shop for those with a taste for finer things.

 S15 5332 BALLARD AVE. NW
206-782-7337

OLIVINE ATELIER *CLOTHING AND SHOES*

This airy boutique painted shades of pink carries what girls want: pretty lingerie, feminine clothes by young designers, shoes, handbags, and Lulu Beauty, Olivine's own line of cosmetics and perfume.

 S14 5344 BALLARD AVE. NW
206-706-4188

SCANDINAVIAN GIFT SHOP *GIFT AND HOME*

In a neighborhood known for its Scandinavian roots, shop owners Solveig and Sverre Hatley offer tradition in the form of miniature trolls, Norwegian sweaters, blue crystal, and wooden clogs. Prices are very reasonable.

 S7 2016 NW MARKET ST.
206-784-9370

SECRET GARDEN BOOKSHOP *BOOKS*

At one time, this decades-old bookshop sold exclusively children's books. The children's collection (and play area) is still extensive, but the store now caters to grown-up reading tastes as well.

 S6 2214 NW MARKET ST.
206-789-5006

OVERVIEW MAP

PRETTY PARLOR *VINTAGE*

Decent prices give way to retro fashions that anyone from Jackie O. to Judy Jetson could adore. Yet Pretty Parlor also gives the latest trends, so hipsters won't be left out in the cold to window-shop.

OVERVIEW MAP A3 6729 GREENWOOD AVE. N.
206-789-8788

 ARTS AND LEISURE

Best local art: **GROVER/THURSTON GALLERY,** p. 61

Best photography: **BENHAM GALLERY,** p. 62

Best glass-blown art: **FOSTER/WHITE GALLERY,** p. 60

Best contemporary art: **HENRY ART GALLERY,** p. 65

Best intimate live music venue: **DIMITRIOU'S JAZZ ALLEY,** p. 68

Best movie house: **SEATTLE CINERAMA THEATRE,** p. 69

Most beautiful theater interior:
THE 5TH AVENUE THEATRE, p. 67

Best large concert hall: **MARION OLIVER MCCAW HALL,** p. 68

Cheapest history lecture/stand-up comedy routine combination:
UNDERGROUND TOUR, p. 73

Best in-city escape from the city: **RAVENNA PARK,** p. 78

Best use of a former industrial area: **GAS WORKS PARK,** p. 76

Best view of Seattle: **KERRY PARK,** p. 75

MUSEUMS AND GALLERIES

MAP 1 PIONEER SQUARE/INTERNATIONAL DISTRIC

BRYAN OHNO GALLERY

Focusing on three-dimensional works and contemporary sculpture, this modern gallery with a specialty in Pacific Rim talent shows such artists as Isamu Noguchi, Marc Katano, and Italo Scanga. The gallery also showcases Chihuly glasswork.

MAP 1 B3 Ⓐ 19   155 S. MAIN ST.
206-667-9572

CAROLYN STALEY FINE PRINTS

The Japanese works exhibited here range from 18th- and 19th-century ukiyo-e woodblocks to sosaku hanga prints from the 1950s to the '80s, in both traditional and personal styles.

MAP 1 B3 Ⓐ 22   314 OCCIDENTAL AVE. S.
206-621-1888

COAST GUARD MUSEUM NORTHWEST

This unusual collection of navigational aids, memorabilia, photographs, and famous ship parts includes a fourth-order lighthouse lens. At one exhibit, you can learn how to monitor ships on Puget Sound.

MAP 1 F1 Ⓐ 40   1519 ALASKAN WAY S.
206-217-6993

DAVIDSON GALLERIES

Prints from the 16th to 21st centuries share this space. The extensive Antique Print Department has catalogued over 5,000 pieces.

MAP 1 B3 Ⓐ 18   313 OCCIDENTAL AVE. S.
206-624-7684

FLURY & COMPANY, LTD.

The vintage photography of Edward S. Curtis, best known for his remarkable portraits of Native Americans, lines plaster walls in this inviting space. Antique Indian art completes the moving collection.

MAP 1 B2 Ⓐ 13   322 1ST AVE. S.
206-587-0260

FOSTER/WHITE GALLERY

This premier spot represents famed glass artist Dale Chihuly and others from his legendary Pilchuck School. Major area painters and sculptors featured include Mark Tobey, Morris Graves, and George Tsutakawa.

MAP 1 B3 Ⓐ 25   123 S. JACKSON ST.
206-622-2833

BRYAN OHNO
GALLERY

G. GIBSON GALLERY

GROVER/THURSTON
GALLERY

G. GIBSON GALLERY

Photographic works by Ansel Adams, Diane Arbus, and the University of Washington's own Imogen Cunningham, as well as various vintage prints and mixed media pieces, are exhibited at this trendy locale.

 A4 **9** 300 S. WASHINGTON ST.
206-587-4033

GREG KUCERA GALLERY

Urbane, provocative art exhibits appear in this prime space, which since 1983 has maintained a solid reputation for showing the work of emerging and renowned artists, including Helen Frankenthaler, Deborah Butterfield, and Robert Motherwell.

 B4 **27** 212 3RD AVE. S.
206-624-0770

GROVER/THURSTON GALLERY

Seattle's largest collection of paintings by Northwest artists, this extensive collection of contemporary art also specializes in modern sculpture. Seattle painters Fay Jones and David Kroll exhibit here.

MAP 1 B3 **21** 309 OCCIDENTAL AVE. S.
206-223-0816

HOWARD HOUSE

This gallery highlights conceptually rigorous works – not just decoration – according to Billy Howard, who arranges shows with pieces by artists featured in other museums (including New York's Whitney).

MAP 1 A3 **5** 604 2ND AVE.
206-256-6399

LINDA HODGES GALLERY

Established in 1983, this big space with a small cadre of artists centers on nationally recognized West Coast painters, such as Gaylen Hansen, Robert Helm, and Roy de Forest.

MAP 1 B2 **14** 316 1ST AVE. S.
206-624-3034

SEATTLE METROPOLITAN POLICE MUSEUM

The largest police museum in the western United States, this collection tracks over 140 years of Northwest law enforcement history, with mug shots, Tommy guns, and even an interactive jail cell.

 B3 **24** 317 3RD AVE. S.
206-748-9991

FIRST THURSDAYS

Seattle's arts community overruns Pioneer Square on the first Thursday of every month, when First Thursday Gallery Walks take place 6–9 P.M. Over 35 art venues (including some restaurants and bars) participate in these events, most notably the **Foster/White Gallery (p. 60), Grover/Thurston Gallery (p. 61),** and **Linda Hodges Gallery (p. 61).** These galleries, among others, use this night as an opportunity to debut their newest exhibits, often serving complimentary wine and appetizers. The walk has even prompted such distinguished venues as the **Seattle Art Museum (p. 6), Seattle Asian Art Museum (p. 11),** and **Museum of History and Industry (p. 65)** to offer free admission all day on the first Thursday of every month.

THE WING LUKE ASIAN MUSEUM

Dedicated to pan-Asian culture and history, this award-winning Smithsonian affiliate presents firsthand immigrant testimonies, a replica of an internment camp room, and artifacts from firecrackers to herbs.

MAP 1 B5 A 31 407 7TH AVE. S.
206-623-5124

MAP 2 DOWNTOWN

BENHAM GALLERY

Photographic arts fill this gigantic space near the Seattle Art Museum with three simultaneous solo shows. Fine-art photographers who've exhibited here include Jerry Uelsmann and Phil Borges.

MAP 2 D3 A 64 1216 1ST AVE.
206-622-2480

SEATTLE AQUARIUM

See SIGHTS, p. 5.

MAP 2 D2 ✪ 58 1483 ALASKAN WAY
206-386-4320

SEATTLE ART MUSEUM

See SIGHTS, p. 6.

MAP 2 D3 ✪ 60 100 UNIVERSITY ST.
206-654-3100

SOUNDBRIDGE

Explore the ins and outs of symphonic music at this technology-driven learning center. Operated by the Seattle Symphony,

**THE WING LUKE
ASIAN MUSEUM**

THE CENTER FOR WOODEN BOATS

Soundbridge encourages visitors to learn from the experts through interactive exhibits, orchestral instruments, and live performances.

 D3 61   200 UNIVERSITY ST.
206-336-6600

WOODSIDE-BRASETH GALLERY
For four decades, this institution on the second floor of a historic building has retained an impressive inventory of Northwest masters: Mark Tobey, Morris Graves, Paul Horiuchi, and Ginny Ruffner.

 A5 10   1533 9TH AVE.
206-622-7243

MAP 3 | BELLTOWN/QUEEN ANNE

THE CENTER FOR WOODEN BOATS
More than 100 preserved wooden vessels dock at this maritime mecca, including yawls, skiffs, knockabouts, and Indian canoes. Rent a sailboat or rowboat for a ride around Lake Union.

 C5 17   1010 VALLEY ST.
206-382-2628

CENTER ON CONTEMPORARY ART (COCA)
A top spot for experimental, conceptual, and multimedia exhibits, CoCA rotates seasonal collections by contemporary Pacific Northwest artists, and also hosts the occasional fashion show.

 D4 36   410 DEXTER AVE. N.
206-728-1980

THE CHILDREN'S MUSEUM
With nine pint-sized galleries and three hands-on studios, this museum lets kids have fun while learning about health, nature, and global culture. There is even a special showroom for toddlers age three and under.

 D3 27   SEATTLE CENTER HOUSE, LOWER LEVEL
206-441-1768

EXPERIENCE MUSIC
PROJECT

HISTORY HOUSE

EXPERIENCE MUSIC PROJECT
See SIGHTS, p. 8.

 MAP 3 D3 ✪28   325 5TH AVE. N.
206-367-5483

PACIFIC SCIENCE CENTER
See SIGHTS, p. 9.

MAP 3 E3 ✪43   200 2ND AVE. N.
206-443-2001

ROQ LA RUE GALLERY
This "Purveyor of Fine Pop Surrealism," devoted to colorful, symbolic, and emotionally charged artists, shows unusual (and just plain weird) works from lowbrow and outsider genres not exhibited elsewhere.

 MAP 3 F3 ♠56   2316 2ND AVE.
206-374-8977

SCIENCE FICTION MUSEUM AND HALL OF FAME
Sharing the Frank Gehry building with the EMP, the world's first sci-fi museum showcases such out-of-this-world artifacts as Captain Kirk's original command chair and Darth Vader's *Empire Strikes Back* helmet.

MAP 3 D3 ♠29   325 5TH AVE. N.
206-724-3428

MAP 4 | CAPITOL HILL

BALLARD FETHERSTON GALLERY
This contemporary gallery shows an arresting collection of narrative, figurative, and abstract works by exceptional local and national talent. Seattle painters Deborah Bell, Michael Schultheis, and Benton Peugh exhibit here.

 MAP 4 F2 ♠36   818 E. PIKE ST.
206-322-9440

MARTIN-ZAMBITO FINE ART
WPA project works and Depression-era prints are the specialty here. The transplanted New Yorker owners also revived the artwork of

once prominent Northwest women, as well as Japanese Americans and other ethnic minorities.

 F2 **37** 721 E. PIKE ST.
206-726-9509

SEATTLE ASIAN ART MUSEUM
See SIGHTS, p. 11.

 B4 **7** 1400 E. PROSPECT ST.
206-654-3100

 MAP 5 | FREMONT/WALLINGFORD

HISTORY HOUSE
After entering through an unusual ironwork gate and sculpture courtyard, learn what shaped Seattle's neighborhoods. Community groups create exhibits with kiosks, slides, and artwork recounting relevant stories from the past.

 D3 **30** 790 N. 34TH ST.
206-675-8875

 MAP 6 | UNIVERSITY DISTRICT

BURKE MUSEUM OF NATURAL HISTORY AND CULTURE
See SIGHTS, p. 14.

 A3 **11** UNIVERSITY OF WASHINGTON, 45TH ST. NE AND 17TH AVE. NE
206-543-5590

HENRY ART GALLERY
Avant-garde shows and contemporary retrospectives show beautifully in this expanded atrium space. A permanent collection of 20,500 works includes paintings, photography, and costumes.

 B3 **17** 15TH AVE. NE AND NE 41ST ST.
206-543-2280

MUSEUM OF HISTORY & INDUSTRY (MOHAI)
The repository of Seattle's past holds Boeing's first airmail seaplane, fun 1962 World's Fair artifacts, and an immense photo collection recording Seattle's major events. First Thursday of the month is free.

 D4 **24** 2700 24TH AVE. E.
206-324-1126

OVERVIEW MAP

FRYE ART MUSEUM
The pleasing collection of pioneer couple Charles and Emma Frye showcases 19th- and early 20th-century paintings, including works

by Andrew Wyeth, John Singer Sargent, and Mary Cassatt, in an intimate modern space. Free admission.

OVERVIEW MAP **E4**   704 TERRY AVE.
206-622-9250

NORDIC HERITAGE MUSEUM

The only collection in the United States honoring immigrants from the five Scandinavian countries, the Nordic Heritage Museum educates visitors through display galleries, cultural shows, and seasonal festivals.

OVERVIEW MAP **A2**   3014 NW 67TH ST.
206-789-5707

ODYSSEY MARITIME DISCOVERY CENTER

More than 40 interactive demonstrations cover seaworthy industries from freighters to ferries. A virtual kayak trip, simulated cargo-ship crane, and kid-size fishing boat are available for novices of all ages.

OVERVIEW MAP **E4**   2205 ALASKAN WAY
206-374-4000

PERFORMING ARTS

 MAP 1 PIONEER SQUARE/INTERNATIONAL DISTRICT

NORTHWEST ASIAN AMERICAN THEATRE (NWAAT) *THEATER*
NWAAT produces thoughtful new works by Asian American writers, producers, and actors. It also brings in performers from Asia and hosts thematic film festivals in its snug but comfortable space.

 MAP 1 B5 **○32** 409 7TH AVE. S.
206-340-1445

 MAP 2 DOWNTOWN

BENAROYA HALL *CONCERTS*
Built for symphonic sound, Seattle Symphony's home also boasts a diverse lineup of return guests like Itzhak Perlman, Bill Cosby, and Wynton Marsalis.

 MAP 2 C3 **○49** 200 UNIVERSITY ST.
206-215-4747

A CONTEMPORARY THEATRE (ACT) *THEATER*
With four theaters downtown, ACT juggles well-honed productions of surefire plays with edgier works by emerging artists. *A Christmas Carol* is reeled out every December for good measure.

 MAP 2 B5 **○32** 700 UNION ST.
206-292-7676

THE 5TH AVENUE THEATRE *THEATER*
The jaw-dropping Chinese-style interior here can make it hard to keep your eyes on the stage, which mounts musicals on their way to and from Broadway.

 MAP 2 C4 **○51** 1308 5TH AVE.
206-625-1418

THE MOORE THEATRE *THEATER*
This 1907 former vaudeville house now hosts indie concerts, off-Broadway theater productions, and dance performances. Beware of the aging, tight-fitting seats upstairs; for more comfort, choose the main floor.

 MAP 2 B2 **○14** 1932 2ND AVE.
206-682-1414 (RECORDED INFORMATION LINE); 206-467-5510

PARAMOUNT THEATRE *VARIOUS*

Staging top music, dance, theater, and comedy acts, this 1928 the-ater also pays frequent homage to its early days by screening silent movies accompanied by live organ music.

MAP 2 A5 🅐9 911 PINE ST.
206-682-1414 (RECORDED INFORMATION LINE); 206-467-5510

TOWN HALL SEATTLE *CONCERTS*

This 900-seat Romanesque theater is a welcome midsize home for readings and classical, jazz, and world music concerts. Town Hall also has a civic bent, organizing forums on current events.

MAP 2 C6 🅐56 1119 8TH AVE.
206-652-4255

MAP 3 BELLTOWN/QUEEN ANNE

BOOK-IT REPERTORY THEATRE *THEATER*

Living up to its "See the Book" slogan, this company in residence at the Seattle Center House brings great literature to the stage with the hope of getting audiences to read more.

MAP 3 D3 🅐32 SEATTLE CENTER, 305 HARRISON ST.
206-216-0833

CONSOLIDATED WORKS *VARIOUS*

A multidisciplinary lab for contemporary art, ConWorks offers drama, art, themed film-and-lecture series, and a theater festival where works are written and staged within 48 hours.

MAP 3 D5 🅐38 500 BOREN AVE. N.
206-381-3218

DIMITRIOU'S JAZZ ALLEY *JAZZ*

Legends like Oscar Peterson and McCoy Tyner, smooth jazz giants like David Sanborn, and funkmasters Tower of Power have all played under the lights at this spacious yet intimate venue.

MAP 3 F4 🅐70 2033 6TH AVE.
206-441-9729

INTIMAN THEATRE *THEATER*

The stately Intiman mounts elegant versions of modernist classics and prominent contemporary works. Its series of American works included *Our Town* and *Grapes of Wrath*.

MAP 3 D2 🅐24 201 MERCER ST.
206-269-1900

KEY ARENA *CONCERTS*

When only the biggest venue will do, stars like Luciano Pavarotti, Bob Dylan, and Nelly play at the Sonics' home court. No other in-city theater approaches its 17,000 seats.

MAP 3 D2 🅐26 SEATTLE CENTER, 305 HARRISON ST.
206-684-7200

MARION OLIVER MCCAW HALL *OPERA/BALLET*

This home of the Seattle Opera and Pacific Northwest Ballet boasts

INTIMAN THEATRE   RE-BAR

a five-story serpentine glass lobby, 2,900 seats, and wonderful acoustics. Big tours like Olivia Newton-John and BB King also use this gorgeous space.

 D3 ⓐ33 SEATTLE CENTER, 305 HARRISON ST.
206-684-7200 (MCCAW HALL); 206-389-7676 (OPERA TICKETS); 206-441-2424 (BALLET TICKETS)

911 MEDIA ARTS CENTER *MOVIE HOUSE*
This arts center offers top-drawer training for the region's film, video, and multimedia artists. Its screenings display the work of young and established filmmakers from around the world.

 D4 ⓐ37 902 9TH AVE. N.
206-682-6552

ON THE BOARDS *VARIOUS*
On the Boards is home to experimental dance, theater, and their many hybrid offspring. In addition to traveling troupes, OTB produces a curated "workshop" of emerging work by local performers.

 C2 ⓐ14 100 W. ROY ST.
206-217-9888

RE-BAR *COMEDY*
Re-bar, one of Seattle's favorite gay-friendly dance clubs, is also home to manic cabaret, skit comedy, and campy (often drag) spoofs of theater classics.

 E5 ⓐ45 1114 HOWELL ST.
206-233-9873

SEATTLE CHILDREN'S THEATRE *THEATER*
Housed in the whimsical Charlotte Martin Theatre, SCT puts on big shows for the not-yet-grown. Kids aren't hushed during shows, and after each performance, they get to grill the cast.

 E3 ⓐ42 SEATTLE CENTER, 201 THOMAS ST.
206-441-3322

SEATTLE CINERAMA THEATRE *MOVIE HOUSE*
Paul Allen's restoration of the Cinerama guaranteed a home for widescreen gems from the 1960s and '70s, but day-to-day it shows blockbusters with perfect sound and picture.

 F4 ⓐ69 2100 4TH AVE.
206-441-3080

SUMMER CONCERT SERIES

Despite Seattle's reputation as the Rain City, summers are gorgeous with warm days and sunny, blue skies – perfect weather to brown-bag it and enjoy one of the many outdoor concert offerings. Formerly held at Pier 62/63, **Summer Nights at South Lake Union (p. 70)** features a diverse lineup of artists like Chris Isaak, Linda Ronstadt, and Billy Idol against a backdrop of beautiful city and water views. The series at the **Woodland Park Zoo (p. 13)** spotlights pop, folk, bluegrass, and alternative rock on a large meadow. Outside Seattle, the concerts at Chateau Ste. Michelle Winery (14111 NE 145th St., Woodinville, 425-415-3300) are worth driving northeast of town for: Its sloping lawn is an ideal setting for sipping wine and lounging to the songs of Don Henley or Diana Krall.

SEATTLE REPERTORY THEATRE *THEATER*
Often a play's first Northwest stop after receiving a Tony, the Rep sets high standards for local theater. Watch for the work of local luminary August Wilson here.

 155 MERCER ST.
206-443-2222 OR 877-900-9285

SUMMER NIGHTS AT SOUTH LAKE UNION *CONCERTS*
After 14 years on Pier 62/63, this popular concert series now uses South Lake Union Park as the setting for its 18-odd concerts of the best in pop, R&B, rock, blues, and jazz under the stars.

 3860 TERRY AVE N.
206-281-7788 (SUMMER NIGHTS/ONE REEL)

TEATRO ZINZANNI *DINNER THEATER*
Part Moulin Rouge, part Cirque du Soleil, this zany spectacle involves a five-course gourmet meal and cabaret entertainment by comic waiters, illusionists, aerialists, guest torch singers, magicians, and a most unusual emcee.

 2301 6TH AVE.
206-802-0015

MAP 4 CAPITOL HILL

BROADWAY PERFORMANCE HALL *VARIOUS*
Seattle's first high school now serves as a comfortable catch-all performance space. Beyond hosting concerts and plays, the hall is involved in many of Seattle's countless film festivals.

 1625 BROADWAY
206-325-3113

EGYPTIAN THEATRE *MOVIE HOUSE*
Originally built as a Masonic Temple in 1915, with the ancient theme added in the 1980s, this theatre screens independent, foreign, and restored classic films. A recent renovation updated the sound system, seats, carpet, and air conditioning.

 F2 **⚫33** 805 E. PINE ST.
206-781-5755

NORTHWEST FILM FORUM *MOVIE HOUSE*
A non-profit organization, Northwest Film Forum occupies a 1920s building and features two cinemas that screen an eclectic mix of foreign films, Hollywood classics, and exciting new work from local and international directors.

 F3 **⚫45** 1515 12TH AVE.
206-267-5380

ST. MARK'S EPISCOPAL CATHEDRAL *CONCERTS*
This cathedral's Sunday evening Compline Choir service has attracted a large, youthful audience. The male chorus performs sacred works from many eras.

 A2 **⚫1** 1245 10TH AVE. E.
206-323-0300

THEATER SCHMEATER *THEATER*
It may milk its income from late-night stagings of *The Twilight Zone*, but this fringe troupe is more serious than its name, excelling at crisp productions of classic works.

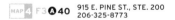 F2 **⚫35** 1500 SUMMIT AVE.
206-324-5801

VELOCITY DANCE CENTER *DANCE*
Top local dancers and choreographers such as Amii LeGendre and KT Niehoff teach classes at Velocity; in turn, the MainSpace draws vibrant performances by young and seasoned artists alike.

 F3 **⚫40** 915 E. PINE ST., STE. 200
206-325-8773

MAP 6 UNIVERSITY DISTRICT

MEANY HALL FOR THE PERFORMING ARTS *VARIOUS*
There is always something exhilarating on the schedule at this elegant and comfortable theater. A globetrotting program of world music and dance, impressive piano recitals, and unsurpassed chamber music are among the various offerings.

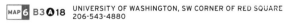 B3 **⚫18** UNIVERSITY OF WASHINGTON, SW CORNER OF RED SQUARE
206-543-4880

THE GRAND ILLUSION CINEMA *MOVIE HOUSE*
Now operated by former employees and volunteers, the longest running independent theater in Seattle still shows the best of indie film, plus classics from filmmakers like Akira Kurosawa, Alfred Hitchcock, and Howard Hawks.
OVERVIEW MAP **B2** 1403 NE 50TH ST.
206-523-3935

SEATTLE PUBLIC THEATER *THEATER*
Productions by this beloved company take the stage of a historic 1928 Greenlake bathhouse. In the 2005 season, *The Complete Works of Shakespeare Abridged* and *Three Tall Women* by Edward Albee were among the choices.
OVERVIEW MAP **A3** 7312 W. GREEN LAKE DR. N. (NEAR STONE AVE. N.)
206-524-1300

TAPROOT THEATRE *THEATER*
This community company in Greenwood maintains its solid reputation for quality productions with fare that includes Ibsen, Thornton Wilder, and The Fantasticks.
OVERVIEW MAP **A3** 204 N. 85TH ST. (JUST WEST OF GREENWOOD AVE. N.)
206-781-9707

VARIOUS LOCATIONS

ANNEX THEATRE *THEATER TROUPE*
Although it lost its Belltown performance space, Annex remains bold and active, continuing to produce wild revivals, documentary theater, and its "Spin the Bottle" cabaret act on different stages. Check the website (www.annextheatre.org) for venue information.
VARIOUS LOCATIONS 206-728-0933

FOOLPROOF FOR THE PERFORMING ARTS *VARIOUS*
Since 1997, this organization has put together scores of diverse events at venues like McCaw Hall and The Paramount. The *American Voices* series brought such speakers as Gore Vidal, Gloria Steinem, and Spike Lee. Check the website (www.foolproof.org) for venue information.
VARIOUS LOCATIONS 206-325-3502

RECREATION

 PIONEER SQUARE/INTERNATIONAL DISTRICT

HING HAY PARK
A colorful dragon mural depicts the history of the International District at this plaza, where Chinese New Year and other Asian holidays are celebrated.

 B5 **33** 423 MAYNARD AVE. S.
206-684-4075

SAFECO FIELD
Locally known as "The Safe," this ballpark keeps Mariners fans dry with its retractable roof. Year-round tours of the ballpark include access to press boxes, luxury seats, and the visitors clubhouse.

 E3 **39** 1250 1ST AVE. S.
206-346-4000

UNDERGROUND TOUR
Explore the underbelly of historic Pioneer Square, where frontier-era rooms lie one floor below ground. Energetic tour guides keep the facts and wisecracks coming.

 A2 **2** 608 1ST AVE. (DOC MAYNARD'S)
206-682-4646

WATERFALL GARDEN PARK
The soothing urban cascade in this corner pocket park is an ideal escape for picnic lunches. United Parcel Service donated the space, which rests on the very spot where the company began.

 B3 **16** 2ND AVE. S. AND S. MAIN ST.
206-624-6096

 DOWNTOWN

ARGOSY CRUISES
Picturesque sites along the harbor, lakes, and locks come alive with narrated anecdotes and highlights, like Bill Gates's mansion and the *Sleepless in Seattle* houseboat. Lunch or dinner is included.

 E2 **72** 1101 ALASKAN WAY, PIER 55
206-623-1445 OR 800-642-7816

SEATTLE ARCHITECTURE FOUNDATION TOURS
Surveys of art-deco skyscrapers and Craftsman bungalows are

WATERFRONT STREETCAR   VOLUNTEER PARK

among the offerings this group organizes. Noon and weekend excursions explore Seattle's theaters, chapels, construction sites, and parks.

 C4 **53** 1333 5TH AVE., LEVEL 3
206-667-9186

SEE SEATTLE WALKING TOURS
Consume munchies at Pike Place Market or history at Pioneer Square; downtown architecture and public art are among the many highlights.

 B3 **26** WESTLAKE PLAZA AT 4TH AVE. AND PINE ST.
(OUTSIDE STARBUCKS)
425-226-7641

TILLICUM VILLAGE
Take a cruise to tiny Blake Island and immerse yourself in Northwest Coast Native culture. The popular two-hour celebration includes traditional dance and a salmon feast, as well as transportation.

 E2 **73** 1101 ALASKAN WAY, PIER 55
206-933-8600

WATERFRONT PARK
This boardwalk sports a fishing pier, a carousel, and a splendid view of Puget Sound attractions. The path leads north to Myrtle Edwards Park.

 D2 **59** 1301 ALASKAN WAY
206-684-4075

WATERFRONT STREETCAR
Not many locals use this vintage trolley, but it's an entertaining way to travel the waterfront from Myrtle Edwards Park to the International District. A day pass allows unlimited stops.

 D2 **57** BROAD ST. AND ALASKAN WAY
206-553-3000

 BELLTOWN/QUEEN ANNE

KENMORE AIR
See Seattle in a unique way – from high above. This popular seaplane

company offers tours to many of the local islands, as well as Victoria, British Columbia.

 C4 **15** 950 WESTLAKE AVE N.
425-486-1257 OR 800-543-9595

KERRY PARK

The breathtaking view from this 1927 donated park space encompasses the Space Needle, downtown skyline, Mount Rainier, and Elliott Bay, visible through circular openings in Doris Chase's sculpture *Changing Form*.

 C1 **13** 211 W. HIGHLAND DR.
206-684-4075

NW OUTDOOR CENTER

Looking for a little offshore adventure? Kayak rentals are available here by the day or the week. Instruction is available for die-hard landlubbers.

 A4 **7** 2100 WESTLAKE AVE. N., STE. 1
206-281-9694 OR 800-683-0637

RIDE THE DUCKS

Splashing in and out of lakes, these WWII amphibious crafts offer fun tours by land and by sea to downtown, Fremont, and the *Sleepless in Seattle* houseboat.

 D3 **35** 516 BROAD ST.
206-441-3825 OR 800-817-1116

MAP 4 | CAPITOL HILL

VOLUNTEER PARK

At the peak of Capitol Hill, this pleasure ground draws large numbers of sunbathers when the weather takes a rare turn toward sunny. It's also home to a conservatory, where cacti, palms, ferns, bromeliads, and orchids are kept at precise temperature and humidity levels.

MAP 4 A3 **2** 1247 15TH AVE. E.
206-684-4555

MAP 5 | FREMONT/WALLINGFORD

BURKE-GILMAN TRAIL

Bike, skate, or jog this 12.5-mile route along an abandoned railway line. Wind through the leafy UW campus past pocket parks, from Lake Union to Lake Washington.

 E5 **32** START NEAR GAS WORKS PARK AT 2101 N. NORTHLAKE WAY
206-684-4075

FREMONT PUBLIC ART WALK

A Lenin statue, a giant troll lurking under a bridge, and a rocket ship are among the sculptures on view along the self-guided tour through quirky Fremont. Maps available at street kiosks.

MAP 5 D2 **14** START AT FREMONT PL. N. AND 36TH ST.
206-632-1500

GAS WORKS PARK LAKE UNION HOUSEBOATS WOODLAND PARK
ROSE GARDEN

GAS WORKS PARK

This former industrial site is now a 20-acre lakeside playground
with fascinating old pipes and pumps and a striking downtown view.
Climb the kite knoll to find the unique sundial.

MAP 5 E5 33 2101 N. NORTHLAKE WAY
206-684-4075

LAKE UNION HOUSEBOATS

Landlubbers can see a few of Seattle's famous houseboats from
Westlake Avenue North, Gas Works Park in Fremont, and Fairview
Avenue on the east side of Lake Union. For those who want to check
out the dwellings from a closer vantage point, Argosy Cruises con-
ducts lake tours that show off the fancier domiciles.

MAP 5 F4 34 ARGOSY CRUISE MARINA, DOCK E, AT WESTLAKE AVE. N.
AND HIGHLAND DR.
206-623-1445 OR 800-642-7816

WOODLAND PARK ROSE GARDEN

Smell the 280 varieties of roses in this 78-year-old garden of climb-
ers, miniatures, and hybrid teas blanketing 2.5 acres. It's one of 24
locations that tests roses in the United States.

MAP 5 A3 2 700 N. 50TH ST.
206-684-4863

MAP 6 | UNIVERSITY DISTRICT

FOSTER ISLAND WALK

Hike this protected marshy wetland to assorted picnic spots, where
herons, ducks, and fish play and boats float by. There's an instructive
interpretive trail, but also a noisy freeway overhead.

MAP 6 D4 23 START AT THE MOHAI PARKING LOT (2700 24TH AVE. E.)

UNIVERSITY DISTRICT PUBLIC ART TOUR

This stroll around the colorful U Dub neighborhood starts at Christie
Park and takes in Greek Row, SAFECO Fountain, Peace Park, and a
whimsical statue of Bigfoot. Call for self-guided maps.

MAP 6 B2 6 START AT NE 43RD ST. AND 9TH AVE. NE
206-684-7171

SPLASHING AROUND SEATTLE

Seattle's watery location makes it quite a playground for urban water activities – despite the often wet weather. The lakes and bays beckon kayakers, while island cruises may appeal to those seeking less heart-pounding diversions. **NW Outdoor Center (p. 75)** offers classes that develop various paddling skills and leads sunset and full-moon kayaking trips as well. A number of waterfront and lake cruises are available through **Argosy Cruises (p. 73),** and Washington State's own **ferries (p. 7)** provide access to nearby islands. And if your watersports preferences tend toward slurping oysters overlooking Puget Sound, opt for a table at **Ray's Boathouse (p. 34).**

UNIVERSITY OF WASHINGTON WATERFRONT ACTIVITIES CENTER

Rent a canoe, rowboat, or kayak to explore the lily-padded waters of Foster Island's wetlands or to float along the shores of Lake Washington.

 D4 ◐ 22   BEHIND HUSKY STADIUM, OFF MONTLAKE BLVD.
206-543-9433

OVERVIEW MAP

DISCOVERY PARK

See SIGHTS, p. 18.

OVERVIEW MAP **B1**   3801 W. GOVERNMENT WAY
206-386-4236

GREEN LAKE PARK

This small lake – a central location for bicyclists, joggers, and in-line skaters – was created when the glaciers retreated. Boat rentals are available at the north end of the lake during summer months.

OVERVIEW MAP **A4**   7201 E. GREEN LAKE DR. N.
206-684-4075

GREGG'S GREEN LAKE CYCLE

Get gear such as bikes, in-line skates, or even jogging strollers at this popular rental facility near Green Lake Park. Open daily year-round.

OVERVIEW MAP **A4**   7007 WOODLAWN AVE. NE
206-523-1822

INTERBAY GOLF CENTER

A state-of-the-art driving range, pro shop, miniature golf, and a nine-hole course await the golf enthusiast. Just five minutes from downtown, this range is one of the finest in Seattle.

OVERVIEW MAP **C3**   2501 15TH AVE W.
206-285-2200

MAGNUSON PARK/ART WALK

Public art abounds at this North Seattle park. Check out the orca fins and the *Soundgarden* – a sculpture that makes use of Mother Nature's breezes to produce wonderful tunes.

OVERVIEW MAP A6 7400 SAND POINT WAY NE
206-684-4946

RAVENNA PARK

Inside these old-growth woods created by landscapers John and Frederick Olmsted, civilization seems far away. Cedars and firs soar above 52 acres of fern-lined paths rambling past creeks and picnickers. An oasis in suburbia.

OVERVIEW MAP B5 5520 RAVENNA AVE. NE
206-684-4075

SHILSHOLE BAY MARINA

The Northwest's largest marina is a favorite hangout for yachts and dinghies, seals, and sea lions. Walk north along Golden Gardens' sandy beach for stunning sunset views.

OVERVIEW MAP A1 7001 SEAVIEW AVE. NW
206-728-3006

VARIOUS LOCATIONS

CHINATOWN DISCOVERY TOURS

Absorbing cultural walks through the International District offer both factual and culinary education: Depending on your appetite, you can nibble your way through Chinatown or enjoy a full eight-course banquet. Reservations required.

STARTING POINTS VARY DEPENDING ON TOUR 425-885-3085

HOTELS

Trendsetter favorite: **THE ACE HOTEL,** p. 83

Most romantic hotel: **ALEXIS HOTEL,** p. 80

Where locals would stay: **HOTEL ÄNDRA,** p. 83

Most unique experience: **PANAMA HOTEL,** p. 80

Best views: **THE EDGEWATER,** p. 83

Best you-only-live-once splurge: **SORRENTO HOTEL,** p. 86

PRICE KEY

$	ROOMS UNDER $200
$$	ROOMS $200-300
$$$	ROOMS OVER $300

MAP 1 PIONEER SQUARE/INTERNATIONAL DISTRI

BEST WESTERN PIONEER SQUARE HOTEL *QUAINT* $
With a boutique flavor and period decor, this historic brick building
is the only hotel in the heart of Pioneer Square. Wireless Internet
access and continental breakfast are included.

 A2 **H3** 77 YESLER WAY
206-340-1234 OR 800-800-5514

PANAMA HOTEL *QUAINT* $
An exquisite teahouse and art deco staircase mark this unique 1910
Japanese American historic landmark. First-floor rooms with shared
baths are nicely renovated. Tours of the on-site Japanese bathhouse
are also available.

 B5 **H29** 605½ S. MAIN ST.
206-223-9242 OR 206-625-9746

MAP 2 DOWNTOWN

ALEXIS HOTEL *ROMANTIC* $$$
This graceful landmark exudes the intimate geniality of a European
inn, with the amenities of a luxury resort. Sumptuous rooms display
flowers and antiques; some have fireplaces and spa tubs. Fit for
sultans and celebrities are the Miles Davis and John Lennon suites,
which feature the artists' serigraphs.

 E4 **H77** 1007 1ST AVE.
206-624-4844 OR 866-356-8894

FAIRMONT OLYMPIC HOTEL *GRAND* $$$
This lavishly restored 1924 Historic Landmark remains the discerning
traveler's choice. Gilt and crystal chandeliers hang from the ceilings;
spacious guestrooms are perfectly appointed.

MAP 2 C4 **H55** 411 UNIVERSITY ST.
206-621-1700 OR 800-441-1414

GRAND HYATT SEATTLE *CHIC* $$
The Grand Hyatt's 425 rooms boast swank features like electronic
blackout drapes, and the views are great above the 22nd floor.

MAP 2 A5 **H8** 721 PINE ST.
206-774-1234 OR 800-233-1234

HOTEL MONACO *CHIC* $$
From a striking lobby mural to rooms decorated in bright, bold
motifs, this celebrated hotel shows distinctive style. CD players, pet
goldfish (by request), and Southern-inspired cuisine are among the
many extras.

MAP 2 D4 **H66** 1101 4TH AVE.
206-621-1770 OR 800-945-2240

HOTEL VINTAGE PARK *ROMANTIC* $$
Savor the seductive ambience and Washington-wine theme in plush

ALEXIS HOTEL   HOTEL VINTAGE PARK

surroundings, with rooms named after state vineyards. Enjoy complimentary fireside tastings for you, and biscuits for your pooch.

 D5 **Ⓗ69** 1100 5TH AVE.
206-624-8000 OR 800-624-4433

INN AT HARBOR STEPS *CHIC* $
Housed in a posh high-rise apartment building, this friendly property offers guests full breakfasts, afternoon wine receptions, and jetted bathtubs. Residential facilities, such as the basketball court, gym, and movie theater, make it better than home.

 D3 **Ⓗ62** 1221 1ST AVE.
206-748-0973 OR 888-728-8910

INN AT THE MARKET *ROMANTIC* $$
This upscale urban resort presents sophisticated comfort with Biedermeier decor, harbor views, and personal service. Eat dinner at the superlative Campagne restaurant, or try one of the inn's unique dining packages, offered in conjunction with other market eateries.

 C2 **Ⓗ35** 86 PINE ST.
206-443-3600 OR 800-446-4484

MAYFLOWER PARK HOTEL *GRAND* $$
This gem has a boutique feel, with refined rooms and an elegant lobby connected to Westlake Center shops. Andaluca Restaurant and Oliver's Lounge are well-established dining options.

 B3 **Ⓗ25** 405 OLIVE WAY
206-382-6990 OR 800-426-5100

THE PARAMOUNT HOTEL *CHIC* $$
This château-style boutique hotel has appealing rooms and is convenient to downtown shopping. Just off the lobby is Dragonfish, an award-winning Asian fusion restaurant.

 A4 **Ⓗ6** 724 PINE ST.
206-292-9500 OR 800-663-1144

PENSIONE NICHOLS *QUAINT* $
A sweet sign beckons you up a couple of flights to this beguiling inn near Pike Place Market. English antiques beautify the six bright, airy rooms; two have private baths.

 B2 **Ⓗ20** 1923 1ST AVE.
206-441-7125 OR 800-440-7125

W HOTEL   MARQUEEN HOTEL

RENAISSANCE SEATTLE HOTEL *GRAND* *$$*

Traditional taste abounds at this hotel, with polished decor and an indoor rooftop pool. Rooms above the 10th floor have picturesque views.

 MAP 2 D5 🅗 71 515 MADISON ST.
206-583-0300 OR 800-278-4159

THE ROOSEVELT HOTEL *GRAND* *$*

This restored 1929 hotel includes some rooms with separate parlors. It also hosts a jazz piano hour (Wed.-Fri.) in the lobby with music and drinks.

MAP 2 B4 🅗 30 1531 7TH AVE.
206-621-1200 OR 800-663-1144

SEATTLE MARRIOTT WATERFRONT *GRAND* *$$*

This welcome addition to the waterfront offers visitors sweeping views of Elliott Bay within a few blocks of the Pike Place Market.

MAP 2 B1 🅗 12 2100 ALASKAN WAY
206-443-5000 OR 800-455-8254

SHERATON SEATTLE HOTEL AND TOWERS *GRAND* *$$*

This large corporate retreat downtown has lots of sleek finery and loads of perks. Check out the Dale Chihuly artwork in the lobby.

MAP 2 B5 🅗 31 1400 6TH AVE.
206-621-9000 OR 800-325-3535

SUMMERFIELD SUITES BY WYNDHAM *GRAND* *$*

There's no expense spared in these spacious, mostly apartment-style suites. Extras include a heated pool, fitness room, and city views. Choose kitchen cooking or food delivery.

MAP 2 A5 🅗 11 1011 PIKE ST.
206-682-8282 OR 800-996-3426

W HOTEL *CHIC* *$$$*

From the dazzling design of the registration desk to the sleekness of each guestroom, this hotel makes guests feel glitzy by association. The sparkling service at this 26-story addition to Seattle's skyline is exceptional. Other bonuses include Bliss products, down bedding, CDs, and munchie boxes.

 MAP 2 D5 🅗 68 1112 4TH AVE.
206-264-6000 OR 877-946-8357

MAP 3 | BELLTOWN/QUEEN ANNE

THE ACE HOTEL   *CHIC* $
This inn's minimalist decor contrasts with warm hardwood details in a renovated historic building. Mid-20th-century modern furniture and contemporary graffiti are tastefully hip. Private bathrooms cost extra.

MAP 3 F3 ❶ 51   2423 1ST AVE.
206-448-4721

THE EDGEWATER   *GRAND* $$
The Beatles once fished out the window at this waterfront hotel. High-beamed ceilings, stone fireplaces, Polo linens, and rubber duckies invoke a relaxed, mountain-lodge ambience.

MAP 3 F3 ❶ 60   2411 ALASKAN WAY
206-728-7000 OR 800-624-0670

HOTEL ÄNDRA   *CHIC* $$
Colored in chocolate browns and Icelandic blues, the Ändra pays homage to the Scandinavian heritage of many Seattle residents. A trendy place for those who want to be seen while enjoying Face Stockholm products, flat screen televisions, and Tivoli radios.

MAP 3 F4 ❶ 73   2000 4TH AVE.
206-448-8600 OR 800-448-8601

MARQUEEN HOTEL   *QUAINT* $
This 1918 former apartment building combines old-world charm, modern conveniences, and upscale touches. Appealing features include kitchenettes in each room, 10-foot ceilings with cove moldings, and hardwood floors with Persian rugs.

MAP 3 D2 ❶ 21   600 QUEEN ANNE AVE. N.
206-282-7407 OR 888-445-3076

MEDITERRANEAN INN   *QUAINT* $
Just blocks from the Seattle Center, this comfortable neighborhood hotel is perfect for the sports fan and culture enthusiast. Take in a game or a show only steps from your front door.

MAP 3 D2 ❶ 25   425 QUEEN ANNE AVE. N.
206-428-4700 OR 866-525-4700

SILVER CLOUD INN – LAKE UNION   *CHIC* $
Situated right across the street from Lake Union, this comfortable hotel offers spacious rooms for those visiting the biotech companies that dot the area. Others can enjoy the nearby Center for Wooden Boats, or watch seaplanes take off and land on the lake.

MAP 3 C6 ❶ 19   1150 FAIRVIEW AVE. N.
206-447-9500 OR 800-330-5812

VANCE HOTEL   *QUAINT* $
This 1920s historic building, built by lumber magnate Joseph Vance, has a handsome, wood-trimmed lobby with stained-glass windows and a superb location. A 2005 renovation gave it a boutique feel with modern amenities like flat-screen televisions.

MAP 3 F5 ❶ 76   620 STEWART ST.
206-956-8500 OR 877-956-8500

GETAWAY HOTELS

For those who want to escape the city without venturing too far away, three luxury hotels within a short drive of downtown offer a getaway atmosphere without the hassle. Northeast of the city in Woodinville, **Willows Lodge** houses The Herbfarm, which serves nine-course meals made from in-season ingredients foraged from nearby farms. It is consistently ranked one of the top restaurants in the country, so reservations are often required months in advance.

The **Woodmark** is located right on Lake Washington and for art lovers, surrounding Kirkland boasts many fine galleries – all an easy walk from the hotel. A little farther out to the east is **Salish Lodge.** Perched high above the Snoqualmie Falls, the Lodge gives visitors a glimpse of the beautiful Cascade foothills and the breathtaking Falls. All three of these hotels have a spa for additional relaxation.

WILLOWS LODGE   *$$*
14580 NE 145TH ST., WOODINVILLE
425-424-3900 OR 877-424-3930
http://willowslodge.com

THE WOODMARK HOTEL ON LAKE WASHINGTON   *$$$*
1200 CARILLON POINT, KIRKLAND
425-822-3700 OR 800-822-3700
http://thewoodmark.com

SALISH LODGE & SPA   *$$$*
6501 RAILROAD AVE., SNOQUALMIE
425-888-2556 OR 800-272-5474
http://salishlodge.com

WARWICK HOTEL   *GRAND*   *$$*
Roomy quarters with marble baths, balconies, and Space Needle views further enhance the classic atmosphere at this hotel. A health club, pool, and courtesy drop-off transportation downtown are pleasant, personal touches.

MAP **3** F4 **①** 71   401 LENORA ST.
206-443-4300 OR 800-426-9280

THE WESTIN SEATTLE   *GRAND*   *$$*
Both cylindrical towers bustle with business travelers, and the Westin offers them every classy accoutrement imaginable. Unparalleled vistas are especially stunning from westerly rooms on the 20th to 47th floors.

MAP **3** F5 **①** 75   1900 5TH AVE.
206-728-1000 OR 888-627-8513

THE BACON MANSION BED & BREAKFAST   CAPITOL HILL INN

 CAPITOL HILL

THE BACON MANSION BED & BREAKFAST *QUAINT* $
This distinguished Edwardian Tudor with wood paneling, crystal chandeliers, a grand piano, and marble fireplaces provides 11 commodious, antique-filled rooms. Two rooms are in the carriage house.

 B2 **H5** 959 BROADWAY E.
206-329-1864 OR 800-240-1864

CAPITOL HILL INN *ROMANTIC* $
Soak in a two-person tub by a double-sided fireplace in the Sherlock Holmes Suite, or choose another themed room. The rich decor evokes another era at this former Victorian bordello.

 E2 **H17** 1713 BELMONT AVE.
206-323-1955

GASLIGHT INN *QUAINT* $
Hang out at the pool or in the parlor of this handsomely furnished, 1906 mission-style house-turned-B&B. Stunning art is well placed throughout; some rooms have a fireplace, deck, or view.

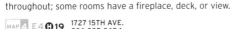 E4 **H19** 1727 15TH AVE.
206-325-3654

HILL HOUSE BED AND BREAKFAST *ROMANTIC* $
Relish gourmet breakfasts and garden suites of chintz, tapestry, and fresh flowers in these suitably enchanting 1903 Victorians.

 D3 **H16** 1113 E. JOHN ST.
206-720-7161 OR 800-720-7161

MILDRED'S BED & BREAKFAST *QUAINT* $
Four antique-appointed rooms and full breakfasts are the charms of this turreted Victorian, which opened in 1982. Stroll the residential neighborhood or appreciate Volunteer Park from the wraparound veranda.

 B4 **H8** 1202 15TH AVE. E.
206-325-6072 OR 800-327-9692

SALISBURY HOUSE *ROMANTIC* $
Scandinavian antiques enhance this 1904 prairie-style property, as do oak writing desks and sleigh beds. A honeymoon favorite,

the lower level suite has a private entry offering even more intimate quarters.

 C4 9 750 16TH AVE. E.
206-328-8682

MAP 5 FREMONT/WALLINGFORD

CHELSEA STATION ON THE PARK *QUAINT* $
Sip cider, feast on hearty breakfasts, and enjoy mountain, garden, or Woodland Park views from nine comfortable rooms housed in two 1929 brick Federal homes.

 A3 3 4915 LINDEN AVE. N.
206-547-6077 OR 800-400-6077

MAP 6 UNIVERSITY DISTRICT

BEST WESTERN UNIVERSITY TOWER HOTEL *CHIC* $
Formerly the Edmond Meany, this hotel has retained its art deco design, retro-hip feel, and panoramic views from its corner rooms.

 A2 3 4507 BROOKLYN AVE. NE
206-634-2000 OR 800-899-0251

COLLEGE INN *QUAINT* $
Family-style quarters take up the second to fourth floors of this rustic Tudor, listed on the National Historic Register. With professors and students rubbing shoulders, Café Allegro and The College Inn pub serve as perfect spots to relive co-ed days.

 B2 16 4000 UNIVERSITY WAY NE
206-633-4441

WATERTOWN *CHIC* $
This hotel near UW has nautical-themed decor and a clever concept: free à la "cart" amenities (the "party cart," the "spa cart"), delivered upon request.

 A2 9 4242 ROOSEVELT WAY NE
206-826-4242 OR 866-944-4242

OVERVIEW MAP

SORRENTO HOTEL *GRAND* $$$
Since 1909, the Sorrento's guests have enjoyed exquisite opulence, from the fountain entry to the mahogany-paneled fireside lounge. Seventy-six sumptuous rooms boast exquisite accommodations.

OVERVIEW MAP **E4** 900 MADISON ST.
206-622-6400 OR 800-426-1265

CITY ESSENTIALS

SEATTLE-TACOMA AIRPORT

The Seattle-Tacoma Airport (206-433-5388 or 800-426-7817, www.portseattle.org), 14 miles south of the city, offers several ways to get into the city. The visitors information desk near baggage claim points travelers to bus stops, taxi stands, shuttle pick-up, and rental car counters.

City buses to the downtown area leave the airport every 30 minutes daily. Check out http://transit.metrokc.gov or call 206-BUS-TIME for times and schedules.

The cost for a trip downtown by taxi runs $30-35, and a $25 flat rate is offered from most downtown hotels to the airport for a 30- to 45-minute ride.

The Gray Line Airport Shuttle (206-626-6088 or 800-426-7532, www.graylineofseattle.com) offers the least expensive trip to select downtown hotels for $8.50 for adults and $6 for children one-way or $14 for adults and $10 for children round-trip. An additional $2.50 one-way or $5 round-trip connects to several other locations. It's approximately a 45-minute ride and leaves every 30 minutes.

Other door-to-door, share-a-ride vans range in price from $21 (downtown hotels) to about $29 for surrounding areas. Reservations are required prior to departure and extra time is necessary for passenger pickups.

SHUTTLE EXPRESS: 425-981-7000 or 800-487-7433

WEST COAST EXPRESS: 206-242-1200

EMERALD CITY: 206-622-3400 or 888-622-3400

DRIVING AND RENTING A CAR

Driving downtown is not recommended or necessary, though a car helps in visiting other neighborhoods. Driving on streets in outlying neighborhoods is less problematic. The main highway, Interstate 5, divides Seattle's east and west. The ship canal cuts the city in half, creating sections designated directionally – north-west, southeast, etc. Driving to most parts of Seattle takes around 15-30 minutes, even if slowed by drawbridges opening for boats.

Most major rental car companies are located at the airport

terminal, though Dollar, Thrifty, and Enterprise involve a shuttle to remote car lots.

The main arterial from the Seattle-Tacoma Airport to the city is Interstate 5. Rush hour traffic congestion can result in one-hour delays; otherwise it's usually a 30-minute drive. To avoid an additional 10 percent airport concession fee, rent a vehicle from a hotel. Many car rental offices are downtown.

BUDGET: 800-527-0700

ENTERPRISE: 800-736-8222

HERTZ: 800-654-3131

NATIONAL: 800-328-4567

PARKING

The main arterials in Seattle neighborhoods are metered at $0.25 per 10–15 minutes, but it's often tough to grab a spot. Garages and lots vary in price from $3 an hour to $15 a day and up. Pay by credit, ATM, or cash. Some streets offer 1–2 hours free parking. Side streets in residential districts are unmarked. Signs list prohibited parking times.

PUBLIC TRANSPORTATION

Seattle's Metro bus system is reliable, reasonably priced, and comprehensive with convenient routes around town. Passengers ride free downtown 6 A.M.–7 P.M. everyday. During other times downtown and to get to other parts of the city, the cost is $1.25–2 for adults or $0.25–0.50 reduced fare. A transfer is good for a return within two hours. During inclement weather, try the underground bus tunnel to cross downtown.

The Metro system (206-BUS-TIME or 800-542-7876, http://transit.metrokc.gov) outlines specific trip options online. Other forms of transportation include the ferry and the waterfront trolley.

The Seattle Center Monorail (206-905-2620, visit www.seattlemonorail.com) makes a quick trip to and from the Seattle Center via the Westlake Mall downtown. Adult fare is $1.50 one-way or $3 round-trip; youth, senior and reduced-fare tickets are $0.75 one-way or $1.50 round-trip. The monorail runs Monday–Thursday 11 A.M.–7 P.M., Fridays 11 A.M.–9 P.M., Saturdays 9 A.M.–9 P.M., and Sundays 9 A.M.–7 P.M. The monorail makes a complete round-trip every 10 minutes.

TAXIS

Except at the airport and hotels, it's troublesome to hail a cab on the street. Call ahead to assure a quick pickup. The flag drop fee is $1.80 and rates run $1.80 per mile.

FARWEST TAXI: 206-622-1717

ORANGE CAB: 206-522-8800

YELLOW AND REDTOP CAB: 206-282-8222 or 206-782-TAXI

VISITOR INFORMATION

Seattle's Convention and Visitors Bureau offers maps and brochures on Seattle sights and attractions. Reservations for hotels, restaurants, and events can also be made there.

SEATTLE'S CONVENTION AND VISITORS BUREAU

`MAP 2` A5   701 PIKE ST., MAIN FL.
206-461-5888 OR 800-535-7071
WWW.SEESEATTLE.ORG.

WEATHER

Seattle's reputation for relentless rain belies its rather temperate climate. The skies are often overcast and drizzly, with the average rainfall at 37 inches annually, and most of it between October and April. Bring light rain gear and wear a rain hat. Locals rarely use umbrellas, except during the occasional squall. "Sunbreaks" are frequent, usually an hour or so prior to sunset. Snow usually comes a couple times in winter, when the steep streets are impossible to navigate for a few days. Temperatures are moderate, hovering around 45°F in the winter, 75°F in the summer, and the rest of the year in the 50s and 60s.

HOURS

While Seattle isn't an especially late-night town, it doesn't roll up the streets at midnight. Action may start earlier with happy hours. (Monday–Wednesday is quieter.) The young and hip bars and clubs in Pioneer Square, Belltown, and Capitol Hill usually serve liquor until 2 A.M. There are a few 24-hour eateries – 13 Coins (125 Boren Ave. N., 206-682-2513) is a favorite.

FESTIVALS AND EVENTS

FEBRUARY

Seattle Festival of Improv Theater: Improv theater groups from all over the country present performances and classes at this multiday event. Mid-February. (University Theater, 5510 University Way NE and additional venues around Seattle, 206-781-3952, www.seattleimprov.com)

MAY

Seattle International Children's Festival: This family-oriented festival features performances by artists from all over the world. Early–mid-May. (Seattle Center, 206-684-7338, www.seattleinternational.org)

Northwest Folklife Festival: This four-day celebration of cultural diversity offers a variety of ethnic food, music, and more. Memorial Day weekend. (Seattle Center, 206-684-7300, www.nwfolklife.org)

Seattle International Film Festival: Hundreds of new, classic, rare, and foreign films are shown in this large cinematic festival. Mid-May–mid-June. (Various venues throughout Seattle, 206-324-9997, www.seattlefilm.com)

JUNE

Solstice Parade and Fremont Fair: Fanciful floats, giant puppets, and more entertain onlookers at this annual event marking summer's arrival. June. (Parade route follows N. 36th St., 206-694-6706, www.fremontfair.com)

Seattle LGBT Pride Parade and Celebration: Thousands take to the streets for this Seattle party celebrating sexual diversity. Weekend in late June. (Broadway Ave. and Pike St. to Volunteer Park, 206-322-9561 or 877-722-9561, www.seattlepride.org)

JULY

Family Fourth: One of Seattle's biggest fireworks displays, this event draws large crowds every year. July 4. (Gas Works Park, 206-281-7788, www.familyfourth.org)

Fourth of Jul-Ivars: This is one of the country's oldest private fireworks celebrations, started by local legend Ivar Haglund. July 4. (Myrtle Edwards Park, 206-587-6500, www.keepclam.com)

Bite of Seattle: Try everything from salmon burgers to alligator-on-a-stick at this culinary festival. Weekend in late July. (Seattle Center, 425-283-5050, www.biteofseattle.com)

Seafair: This city-wide, month-long salute to summer features parades, hydroplane racing, food festivals, and more. July-August. (Various locations, 206-728-0123, www.seafair.com)

SEPTEMBER

Bumbershoot: More than 2,500 artists, including musicians, comedians, filmmakers, and more, participate in this festival every year. Labor Day weekend. (Seattle Center, 206-281-7788, www.bumbershoot.org)

OCTOBER

Earshot Jazz Festival: This festival features performances and classes by notable jazz musicians from all over the world. October-November. (Various locations, 206-547-6763, www.earshot.org)

NOVEMBER

Winterfest: This winter holiday celebration features food, family activities, concerts, and exhibits. Day after Thanksgiving-December 31. (Seattle Center, 206-684-7200, www.seattlecenter.com)

Bon-Macy's Holiday Parade: This parade includes fireworks and the lighting of the downtown Christmas tree and Bon-Macy's Star. Late November. (Downtown Seattle, 206-506-6000, www.macys.com)

DECEMBER

New Year's Eve at the Space Needle: The world's tallest structure-launched fireworks show boasts more than 2,000 pyrotechnic effects. December 31. (Seattle Center, 206-905-2100, www.spaceneedle.com)

DISABLED ACCESS

Seattle is perhaps one of the best cities for people with disabilities to live in. Services are readily available in most buildings, and public toilets and buses are wheelchair accessible. However, steep hilly streets, particularly downtown, are somewhat challenging for travelers with disabilities. The elevator at the Pike Place Market is helpful, and the underground bus tunnel makes crossing downtown easier. Museum parking lots and many restaurants have designated disabled parking spaces.

SAFETY

Downtown Seattle streets are alive with people walking around at night, providing a feeling of security and comfort. In general, Seattle is a safe city, but as it has grown, so has its crime rate. Common sense is required to avoid being a target. Be aware of your belongings at all times and keep your vehicles locked. Transients hanging out in Pioneer Square are fairly harmless. Be alert during late evenings when the area's bars and clubs shut down.

HEALTH AND EMERGENCY SERVICES

In case of a medical emergency or fire, call 911. For urgent medical attention without the assistance of an ambulance, the following medical centers offer emergency care.

HARBORVIEW MEDICAL CENTER
MAP 1 A5 325 9TH AVE.
206-731-3074

SWEDISH MEDICAL CENTER
MAP 7 B2 5300 TALLMAN AVE. NW
206-782-2700

VIRGINIA MASON
MAP 2 C6 925 SENECA ST.
206-624-1144

UNIVERSITY OF WASHINGTON MEDICAL CENTER
MAP 6 C3 1959 NE PACIFIC ST.
206-598-3300

PHARMACIES

BARTELL DRUGS
MAP 1 A2 600 1ST AVE. N.
206-284-1353

MAP 2 B4 1628 5TH AVE.
206-622-0581

RITE AID
MAP 6 A2 4535 UNIVERSITY WAY NE
206-632-3975

MEDIA AND COMMUNICATIONS

Seattle's two daily newspapers, *The Seattle Times* and the *Seattle Post-Intelligencer,* provide world and local news. The city's two free weeklies, *Seattle Weekly* and *The Stranger,* cover local news and have entertainment listings every Thursday.

The main area code in Seattle is 206. Some local toll calls have prefixes 425 (east and north) and 253 (south).

Public pay phones can be difficult to find on the street, though most public buildings, hotel lobbies, and restaurants have phone booths. Local calls cost $0.50. Calling cards are recommended for long-distance calls.

Mobile phones are commonplace in Seattle, but considerate etiquette is required. Some restaurants won't even allow usage. Reminders to turn mobile phones off are announced at theaters and public performances.

In Seattle's downtown, the main post office is located at 301 Union Street, and is open Monday–Friday 7:30 A.M.–5:30 P.M. For additional locations, call the United States Postal Service hotline at 800-275-8777.

INTERNET

Hotels are moving toward offering business centers with WI-FI (wireless Internet access), and some include rooms with high-speed data ports. Kinko's Copies, located in most neighborhoods, provides Internet and late-night computer services. For Internet access and a latte, try the following cyber cafés.

AURAFICE INTERNET CAFE
MAP 4 F2 616 E. PINE ST.
206-860-9977

ONLINE COFFEE COMPANY
MAP 2 E3 1111 1ST AVE.
206-381-1911

SMOKING

Although smoking is prohibited in public buildings, it is still permitted in most clubs, bars, and restaurants in the city.

TIPPING

Restaurant wait staff, bartenders, and taxi drivers should be tipped 15-20 percent of the total. Porters and skycaps should be tipped $1-2 per bag. Since tips compensate for low salaries, consider the quality of service to determine how much is an adequate token of appreciation.

DRY CLEANERS

CREASES
MAP 3 F3 1822 TERRY AVE.
206-382-9265

ROYAL CLEANERS
MAP 4 F4 1406 E. PIKE ST.
206-324-7401

STREET INDEX

NUMBERED STREETS

1st Ave.: Map 1 A2; Map 2 B1, D3; Map 3 E3

1st Ave. N: Map 3 A2, C2; Map 5 E2

1st Ave. NE: Map 5 A6, C6

1st Ave. NW: Map 5 A2, B1, B2, C2

1st Ave. S: Overview Map F4; Map 1 B2; Map 2 F4

1st Ave. W: Map 3 A2, C2; Map 5 E1

2nd Ave.: Overview Map D4, E4; Map 1 A3; Map 2 A1, C3; Map 3 E3

2nd Ave. Ext: Map 1 B3

2nd Ave. N: Map 3 A2, B2, C2, E2; Map 5 E2

2nd Ave. NE: Map 5 A6, C6

2nd Ave. NW: Map 5 A1, B1, C1

2nd Ave. S: Map 1 B3

2nd Ave. W: Map 3 A1, B1; Map 5 F1

3rd Ave.: Map 1 A3; Map 2 A2, C4; Map 3 E3

3rd Ave. N: Map 3 A3, C3; Map 5 E2

3rd Ave. NW: Overview Map A3; Map 5 B1

3rd Ave. S: Map 1 A3, E4; Map 2 F6

3rd Ave. W: Map 3 A1, B1; Map 5 E1

4th Ave.: Overview Map D4, E4; Map 1 A4; Map 2 A2, C4; Map 3 F4

4th Ave. N: Map 3 A3, C3; Map 5 E3

4th Ave. NE: Map 5 B6, C6; Map 6 A1, B1

4th Ave. NW: Map 5 B1

4th Ave. S: Overview Map F4; Map 1 B4; Map 2 F6

4th Ave. W: Map 3 A1, B1, D1; Map 5 E1

5th Ave.: Map 1 A4; Map 2 A3, C4; Map 3 E4

5th Ave. N: Map 3 A3, B3

5th Ave. NE: Map 5 C6; Map 6 B1

5th Ave. NW: Map 5 A1, B1

5th Ave. S: Map 1 B4

5th Ave. W: Map 3 A1, B1, D1; Map 5 E1

6th Ave.: Map 1 A4; Map 2 C5; Map 3 E4

6th Ave. N: Map 3 C4, D4; Map 5 F3

6th Ave. NW: Map 5 C1

6th Ave. S: Map 1 C5, E5

6th Ave. W: Map 3 A1, B1

7th Ave.: Map 2 B5; Map 3 E4

7th Ave. S: Map 1 C5

8th Ave.: Map 2 B5; Map 3 E5; Overview Map E4

8th Ave. N: Map 3 A4, D4; Map 5 F4

8th Ave. NE: Map 6 A1

8th Ave. NW: Overview Map A3

8th Ave. S: Map 1 C6, F5

9th Ave.: Map 2 C6; Map 3 E5

9th Ave. N: Map 3 D4

9th Ave. NE: Map 6 A2

10th Ave.: Overview Map C3; Map 1 A6; Map 4 D3, F3

10th Ave. E: Map 4 B3; Map 6 D1, F1

10th Ave. S: Map 1 B6

11th Ave.: Map 4 E3

11th Ave. E: Map 4 B3; Map 6 D2, F2

11th Ave. NE: Map 6 A2

11th Ave. NW: Overview Map A3

11th Ave. W: Overview Map C3

12th Ave.: Map 4 E3

12th Ave. E: Map 4 B3; Map 6 F2

12th Ave. NE: Map 6 A2

13th Ave.: Map 4 E3

13th Ave. E: Map 4 C3; Map 6 E2

14th Ave.: Map 4 E4

14th Ave. E: Map 4 B4; Map 6 F2

15th Ave.: Map 4 E4

15th Ave. E: Map 4 B4; Map 6 F2

15th Ave. NE: Overview Map A5; Map 6 A3

15th Ave. NW: Overview Map A3; Map 7

15th Ave. W: Overview Map C3

16th Ave.: Map 4 E4

16th Ave. E: Map 4 B4

17th Ave.: Map 4 E4

17th Ave. E: Map 4 B4

17th Ave. NW: Map 7

18th Ave.: Map 4 E5

18th Ave. E: Map 4 B5

19th Ave.: Map 4 E5

19th Ave. E: Map 4 B5; Map 6 E3

19th Ave. NE: Map 6 A3

20th Ave.: Map 4 E5

20th Ave. E: Map 4 B5; Map 6 E3

20th Ave. NE: Map 6 A3

20th Ave. NW: Overview Map A2; Map 7

21st Ave.: Map 4 E5

21st Ave. E: Map 4 B5

21st Ave. NE: Map 6 A3

21st Ave. W: Map 7

22nd Ave. E: Map 4 B5; Map 6 E4

22nd Ave. NW: Map 7

22nd Ave. W: Map 7

23rd Ave.: Overview Map D5; Map 4 E6

23rd Ave. E: Map 4 B6, C6; Map 6 F4

23rd Ave. S: Overview Map E5

23rd Ave. W: Map 7

24th Ave.: Map 4 E6

24th Ave. E: Map 4 B6, C6; Map 6 F4

24th Ave. NW: Overview Map A2; Map 7

24th Ave. W: Overview Map C2; Map 7

25th Ave.: Map 4 E6

25th Ave. E: Map 4 B6, C6; Map 6 F4

25th Ave. NE: Overview Map A5

26th Ave.: Map 4 E6

26th Ave. E: Map 4 A6, C6; Map 6 F4

26th Ave. NW: Map 7

26th Ave. W: Map 7

27th Ave. W: Map 7

28th Ave. NW:
Overview Map A2;
Map 7

28th Ave. W:
Overview Map C2;
Map 7

28th Pl. W: Map 7

30th Ave. NW: Map 7

30th Ave. W: Map 7

31st Ave. S: Overview
Map E6

31st Ave. W: Map 7

32nd Ave. NW
Overview Map A2;
Map 7

32nd Ave. W: Map 7

33rd Ave. W: Map 7

34th Ave. W:
Overview Map C2

N 34th St.: Map 5 E4

35th Ave. NE:
Overview Map A6

N 35th St.: Map 5 D5

36th Ave. NE: Map
6 A6

N 36th St.: Map 5
D2, D5

37th Ave. NE: Map
6 A6

N 37th St.: Map 5 D5

38th Ave. E: Map
6 E6

N 38th St.: Map 5
D4, D5

NE 38th St.: Map
6 B6

39th Ave. NE: Map
6 A6

39th St.: Overview
Map B3

N 39th St.: Map 5
C2, C5

N 40th St.: Overview
Map B4; Map 5 C5

NE 40th St.: Map 5
C6; Map 6 B1, B2

NW 40th St.: Map 5 C1

N 41st St.: Map 5 C5

NE 41st St.: Map 6
B2, B6

NW 41st St.: Map 5 C1

N 42nd St.: Map 5
C2, C5

NE 42nd St.: Map
5 C6; Map 6 A6,
B1, B2

NW 42nd St.: Map
5 C1

N 43rd St.: Map 5 B2,
B3, B5

NE 43rd St.: Map
5 B6; Map 6 A1,
A2, A6

NW 43rd St.: Map
5 B1

N 44th St.: Map 5 B2,
B3, B4, B5

NE 44th St.: Map 5
B6; Map 6 A1, A6

NW 44th St.: Map
5 B1

45th Ave. NE:
Overview Map A6

N 45th St.: Overview
Map B4; Map 5
B2, B5

NE 45th St.: Map 5
B6; Map 6 A2

NE 45th Pl.: Map
6 A5

NW 45th St.: Map
5 B1

N 46th St.: Overview
Map B4; Map 5
B3, B5

NW 46th St.: Map
5 B1

N 47th St.: Map 5 B3

NE 47th St.: Map 5
B6; Map 6 A6

NW 47th St.: Map 5
B1; Map 7

N 48th St.: Map 5 A3

NW 48th St.: Map
5 A1

N 49th St.: Map 5 A3

NW 49th St.: Map
A1; Map 7

N 50th St.: Overview
Map B4; Map 5 A3

NE 50th St.: Map
5 A6

NW 50th St.: Map 5
A1; Map 7

N 51st St.: Map 5
A2, A5

NE 51st St.: Map 5 A6

NW 51st St.: Map 5 A1;
Map 7

N 52nd St.: Map 5
A5, A6

NE 52nd St.: Map
5 A6

NW 52nd St.: Map 5
A1; Map 7

N 53rd St.: Map 5 A5

NE 53rd St.: Map
5 A6

NW 53rd St.: Map 5
A1; Map 7

NW 54th St.: Map 7

55th Ave. NE:
Overview Map A6

NE 55th St.: Overview
Map B6

NW 56th St.: Map 7

NW 57th St.: Map 7

NW 58th St.: Map 7

NW 59th St.: Map 7

NE 60th St.:
Overview Map B6

NW 60th St.:
Overview Map B2;
Map 7

NW 61st St.: Map 7

NW 62nd St.: Map 7

NW 63rd St.: Map 7

NE 65th St.: Overview
Map A6

NW 65th St.:
Overview Map A2

NE 70th St.: Overview
Map A6

NW 70th St.:
Overview Map A2

NE 75th St.: Overview
Map A6

NW 75th St.:
Overview Map A2

80th St.: Overview
Map A5

NW 80th St.:
Overview Map A2

A

Admiral Way SW:
Overview Map F2

Airport Way S:
Overview Map F5;
Map 1 D4

Alaskan Way:
Overview Map E4,
F4; Map 1 A2; Map
2 E3; Map 3 D1, F2

Alaskan Way S: Map
1 C2

Alaskan Way W: Map
2 C1

Alaskan Way Viaduct:
Map 1 C2; Map
2 D2

Albion Pl. N: Map
5 D3

Alder St.: Map 1 A5

Alki Ave. SW:
Overview Map F2

N Allen Pl.: Map 5
B3, B4

E Allison St.: Map 5
D6; Map 6 D1

Aloha St.: Map 3
C2, C5

E Aloha St.: Overview
Map D5; Map 4
C5, C6

Arboretum Dr. E: Map
6 F5

Armour St.: Map 5 E2

W Armour St.: Map
5 E1

Ashworth Ave. N: Map
5 D4

S Atlantic St.: Map
1 F5

Auburn Pl. E: Map
4 A4

Aurora Ave. N:
Overview Map B4;
Map 3 B4; Map
5 C3

Aurora Bridge: Map
5 E3

B

Bagley Ave. N: Map
5 B5

Baker Ave. NW: Map 5 A1, B1

Ballard Ave. NW: Map 7

Ballard Bridge: Map 7

Barnes Ave. NW: Map 7

W Barrett St.: Map 5 E1

Battery St.: Map 3 F3

Bay St.: Map 3 E2

Beacon Ave. S: Overview Map F5

Bell St.: Map 2 A1; Map 3 F4

Bellevue Ave.: Map 3 C6; Map 4 C1

Bellevue Pl.: Map 3 C6

Belmont Pl. E: Map 4 B2

Belmont Ave.: Map 3 C6; Map 4 B1, C1, E2

NE Belvoir Pl.: Map 6 B6

W Bertona St.: Map 5 D1

Bigelow Ave.: Map 3 A3

Birch Ave.: Map 5 F3

Blaine St.: Map 3 B2

E Blaine St.: Map 3 B6; Map 6 F1, F3

W Blaine St.: Map 3 B1

Blanchard St.: Map 2 A1; Map 3 F4

E Blenheim Dr.: Map 6 F6

NE Boat St.: Map 6 C2

Boren Ave.: Overview Map E5; Map 2 A6; Map 3 E5; Map 4 F1

Boren Ave. N: Map 3 D5

Boston St.: Map 3 A3

E Boston St.: Map 3 A6; Map 6 F1

E Boston Ter.: Map 6 F2

W Boston St.: Map 3 A2

N Bowdoin Pl.: Map 5 C2

NW Bowdoin Pl.: Map 5 C1

Boyer Ave. E: Map 6 D1, F3

Boylston Ave.: Map 4 B2, C2, E2

Boylston Ave. E: Map 5 E6; Map 6 E1

Bridge Way N: Map 5 D3

Broad St.: Overview Map D4; Map 3 E3

Broadmoor Dr. E: Map 6 F6

Broadway: Map 4 E2

Broadway E: Map 1 A6; Map 4 B2; Map 6 C1, D1, E1

Brooklyn Ave. NE: Map 6 A2

NW Brygger Pl.: Map 7

Burke Ave. N: Map 5 A5, B5

C

E Calhoun St.: Map 6 E4

California Ave. SW: Overview Map F2

NE Campus Pky.: Map 6 B2

Canal Rd.: Map 6 B5

NW Canal St.: Map 5 D2

Carr Pl. N: Map 5 D4

Cedar St.: Map 3 F3

S Charles St.: Map 1 D5

Cherry St.: Map 1 A3; Map 2 E5

E Cherry St.: Overview Map E5

Clark Rd.: Map 6 A5

Clay St.: Map 3 E3

Colorado Ave. S: Map 1 F2

Columbia Rd.: Map 6 C3

Columbia St.: Map 1 A2; Map 2 E5

W Commodore Way: Map 7

Comstock Pl.: Map 3 B3

Comstock St.: Map 3 B4

W Comstock St.: Map 3 B1

Corliss Ave. N: Map 5 B5

Coryell Ct. E: Map 4 D5

Crawford Pl.: Map 3 F6; Map 4 F1

W Cremona St.: Map 5 D1

E Crescent Dr.: Map 4 A5

Crockett St.: Map 3 A3, A4

E Crockett St.: Map 6 F2

W Crockett St.: Map 3 A1

D

Dayton Ave. N: Map 5 A2, B2, C2, D2

S Dearborn St.: Overview Map E5; Map 1 C5

Delmar Dr. E: Map 6 E2

Denny Way: Overview Map D4; Map 3 E4

E Denny Way: Map 3 E6; Map 4 E3, E6

Densmore Ave. N: Map 5 A4, C4

Dexter Ave. N: Map 3 A4, B4; Map 5 E3

Dexter Ct.: Map 3 C4

Dilling Way S: Map 1 A4; Map 2 F6

NW Dock Pl.: Map 7

N Dorothy Pl.: Map 5 C4

Douglas Dr.: Map 6 B5

Dravus St. W: Overview Map C2

W Dravus St.: Map 5 D1

E

Eagle St.: Map 3 E2

Eastern Ave. N: Map 5 B6

Eastlake Ave.: Map 3 B6, D6; Map 4 C1

Eastlake Ave. E: Overview Map C4; Map 5 E6, F6; Map 6 D1

E Edgar St.: Map 5 E6; Map 6 D1

Elliott Ave.: Overview Map D3; Map 3 D1, F2

W Emerson St.: Overview Map B1

Etruria St.: Map 5 E1

Evanston Ave. N: Map 5 A2, B2, D2

Everett Ave. E: Map 6 F2

Evergreen Point Floating Bridge: Overview Map C6

W Ewing St.: Map 5 D1

F

Fairview Ave.: Map 3 A6, C5, D5; Map 4 B1

Fairview Ave. E: Map 5 E6, F6; Map 6 D1

Federal Ave.: Map 4 B3

Federal Ave. E: Map 6 E1

E Fir St.: Map 1 A6

Florentia St.: Map 5 E1

W Fort St.: Map 7

Francis Ave. N: Map 5 B2, D2

Franklin Ave. E: Map 5 F6; Map 6 D1, E1

Franklin Pl. E: Map 6 F1

Fremont Ave. N:
Overview Map B4;
Map 5 B3

Fremont Ln. N: Map
5 D3

Fremont Pl. N: Map
5 D3

Fremont Way N: Map
5 D3

Fuhrman Ave. E: Map
6 C1

Fulton St.: Map 5 E2

W Fulton St.: Map 5 E1

G

Galer St.: Overview
Map D3; Map 3 B2

E Galer St.: Map 4 A3,
A5, A6

W Galer St.: Map 3 B1

Garfield St.: Map 3 B2

E Garfield St.: Map 3
B6; Map 4 A1, A3

W Garfield St.: Map
3 B1

Gay Ave. W: Map 7

Gilman Ave. W:
Overview Map B2;
Map 7

Gilman Pl. W: Map 7

E Glen St.: Map 4 E5

Grandview Pl.: Map
4 A4

E Green Lake Way N:
Overview Map B4

E Green Lake Way W:
Map 5 A4, B3

Greenwood Ave.: Map
5 A2

Greenwood Ave. NW:
Overview Map A3

E Gwinn Pl.: Map 6 D1

H

Halladay St.: Map
5 F3

W Halladay St.: Map
5 F1

E Hamlin St.: Map 5
E6; Map 6 D1, D3

Harbor Ave. SW:
Overview Map F3

Harley Ave. W: Map 7

Harrison St.: Map
3 D4

E Harrison St.: Map 3
C6; Map 4 D3

W Harrison St.: Map
3 D2

Harvard Ave.: Map 4
B2, E2

Harvard Ave. E: Map
6 C1, E1

Hayes St.: Map 3 B2

E Helen St.: Map 4 B6

Highland Dr.: Map
3 C2

E Highland Dr.: Map 4
B2, B5

W Highland Dr.: Map
3 C1

S Holgate St.:
Overview Map F4

Homer M Hadley
Memorial Bridge:
Overview Map F6

Howe St.: Map 3 A3

E Howe St.: Overview
Map C5; Map 6
E1, F4

W Howe St.: Map 3 A1

Howell St.: Map 3 F5,
Map 4 E1

E Howell St.: Map
3 E6; Map 4 E2,
E4, E6

Hubbell Pl.: Map 2 A6

IJ

Interlake Ave.: Map
5 B4

Interlaken Blvd.: Map
6 E2, F3

Interlaken Dr.: Map 4
A5, A6

Interlaken Dr. E: Map
6 F3

Interlaken Pl.: Map
4 A6

NW Ione Pl.: Map 7

S Jackson St.:
Overview Map E4;
Map 1 B3

James St.: Overview
Map E4; Map 1 A3;
Map 2 F5

W Jameson St.: Map 7

E Jansen Ct.: Map
4 D5

Jefferson Rd.: Map
6 B4

Jefferson St.: Map 1
A4; Map 2 F6

E John Ct.: Map 4 E4

John St.: Map 3
E2, E4

E John St.: Map 4 D3,
D4, D6

KL

Keystone Pl. N: Map
5 A5

S King St.: Map 1
B3, B5

W Kinnear Pl.: Map
3 C1

Kirkwood Pl. N: Map
5 A5

Lacey V Murrow
Memorial Bridge:
Overview Map F6

Lakeview Blvd.: Map 3
C6; Map 4 B1

Lake Washington
Blvd.: Overview
Map D6; Map 6 F4

S Lander St.:
Overview Map
F4, F5

S Lane St.: Map 1 C5

Latona Ave. NE: Map
5 A6, B6, C6; Map
6 A1

Leary Ave. NW: Map 7

Leary Way NW:
Overview Map B3;
Map 5 C1

Lee St.: Map 3 B3

E Lee St.: Map 4 A6

W Lee St.: Map 3 B1

Lenora St.: Map 2 B1;
Map 3 F4

Linden Ave. N: Map
5 B3

Lorentz Pl. N: Map
5 F2

Loretta Pl.: Map 4 E1

E Louisa St.: Map 5
F6; Map 6 E1, E4

N Lucas Pl.: Map 5 C4

Lynn Ln.: Map 3 A2

E Lynn St.: Map 6
E1, E4

M

Madison St.: Map
2 D5

E Madison St.:
Overview Map D5;
Map 4 D6

Magnolia Blvd. W:
Overview Map C1

S Main St.: Map 1 B4

Malden Ave. E: Map
4 C4

W Mansell St.: Map 7

Marion St.: Map 2 E5

E Marion St.:
Overview Map E5

NW Market St.:
Overview Map B2;
Map 5 A1; Map 7

E Martin St.: Map 6 C1

Martin Luther
King Jr. Way S:
Overview Map D6

Mary Gate S
Memorial Dr.: Map
6 A5

Mason Rd.: Map 6 B4

S Massachusetts St.:
Map 1 F1, F2

Mayfair Ave. N: Map
5 E2

Maynard Ave. S: Map
1 C5

McGilvra Blvd. E:
Overview Map D6

McGraw Pl.: Map 5
F1, F2,

McGraw St.: Overview
Map C3; Map 5 F2

E McGraw St.: Map
6 E4

Melrose Ave.: Map 3 C6; Map 4 C1

Memorial Way: Map 6 A3

Menford Pl.: Map 5 B4

Mercer St.: Overview Map D4; Map 3 D2

E Mercer St.: Map 3 C6; Map 4 C3

W Mercer St.: Map 3 D1

Meridian Ave. N: Overview Map B4; Map 5 B5

Midvale Ave. N: Map 5 C4

N Midvale Pl.: Map 5 B3

E Miller St.: Map 6 E1, E4

Minor Ave.: Map 3 E5, F6; Map 4 E1

Minor Ave. E: Map 3 A6; Map 5 F6

Minor Ave. N: Map 3 C5, D5

Montlake Blvd. NE: Map 6 C4

Montlake Bridge: Map 6 D4

W Montlake Pl. E: Map 6 E3

N Motor Pl.: Map 5 B3

N

Nagle Pl.: Map 4 E3

Newell St.: Map 5 E2

W Newell St.: Map 5 E1

Newton St.: Map 3 A3

E Newton St.: Map 3 A6; Map 6 F1, F4

Nickerson St.: Map 5 D2

Nob Hill Ave.: Map 3 A3, B3, C3

Nob Hill Ave. N: Map 5 E3, F3

Northlake Pl.: Map 6 B1

N Northlake Pl.: Map 5 E4

N Northlake Way: Map 5 D5

NE Northlake Way: Map 6 B1

OPQ

Occidental Ave. S: Map 1 A3, C3

E Olive St.: Map 3 E6; Map 4 E2, E4, E5, E6

Olive Way: Overview Map D4; Map 2 A4; Map 3 F5

E Olive Way: Map 3 E6; Map 4 E1

W Olympic Pl.: Map 3 C1

Oowlitz Rd.: Map 6 B2

Orange Pl. N: Map 3 B2

NE Pacific Pl.: Map 6 C3

N Pacific St.: Map 5 D5

NE Pacific St.: Map 6 B1, C3

Palatine Ave. N: Map 5 A2, B2, C2, D2

Parkside Dr. E: Map 6 F6

Pend Oreille Rd.: Map 6 A4

Phinney Ave. N: Map 5 A2

N Phinney Way: Map 5 B3

Pike Pl.: Map 2 B2

Pike St.: Map 2 C3; Map 3 F5

E Pike St.: Map 3 F6; Map 4 F3, F6

Pine St.: Overview Map E4; Map 2 B3; Map 3 F5

E Pine St.: Map 3 F6; Map 4 F3, F6

S Plummer St.: Map 1 D5

Pontius Ave.: Map 3 D5

Portage Bay Pl. E: Map 6 C1

Post Aly.: Map 2 D3

Post Ave.: Map 1 A2; Map 2 E3

Prefontaine Pl. S: Map 1 A4

Prospect St.: Map 3 C2, C6

E Prospect St.: Map 4 B2, B5

W Prospect St.: Map 3 C1

Queen Anne Ave.: Overview Map D3; Map 3 B2; Map 5 F1, F2

Queen Anne Dr.: Map 5 F2

R

Rainier Ave.: Overview Map F5

NE Ravenna Blvd.: Overview Map B5

Raye St.: Map 5 F3

W Raye St.: Map 5 F1

Republican St.: Overview Map D4; Map 3 D4

E Republican St.: Map 3 C6; Map 4 D3

W Republican St.: Map 3 D1

E Roanoke St.: Map 5 F6; Map 6 E1, E4

Roosevelt Way NE: Overview Map A5; Map 6 A2

Roy St.: Map 3 C2; Map 3 D5

E Roy St.: Map 3 C6; Map 4 C3

W Roy St.: Map 3 C1

Royal Ct.: Map 3 E6

Royal Brougham Way: Overview Map F4

S Royal Brougham Way: Map 1 E3

Russell Ave. NW: Map 7

S

Sand Point Way N: Map 6 A6

Sand Point Way NE: Overview Map B6

Seaview Ave. NW: Overview Map A1

Seneca St.: Overview Map E4; Map 2 D4

E Shelby St.: Map 6 D1, D3

Shenandoah Dr. E: Map 6 F6

Shilshole Ave. NW: Map 7

Smith Pl.: Map 5 F2

Smith St.: Map 5 F3

W Smith St.: Map 5 F1

Spring St.: Map 2 D4

Spruce St.: Map 1 A6

Stevens Way: Map 6 A3, C3

Stewart St.: Overview Map D4; Map 2 B2; Map 3 F5, Map 4 E1

Stone Ave. N: Map 5 A4

Stone Way N: Map 5 C4

Summit Ave.: Map 3 E6; Map 4 E2

Summit Ave. E: Map 3 C6; Map 4 B2, C2

Sunnyside Ave.: Map 5 B5

Surber Dr. NE: Map 6 B6

T

Tallman Ave. NW: Map 7

Taylor Ave. N: Overview Map D4; Map 3 B3, D3

Terrace St.: Map 1 A4; Map 2 F6

Terry Ave.: Map 2 A6; Map 3 E5

Terry Ave. N: Map 3 D5

Thackeray Pl. N: Map 5 B6

Thomas St.: Map 3 D4

E Thomas St.: Overview Map D5; Map 3 C6; Map 4 D3, D4, D6

W Thomas St.: Map 3 D2

Thorndyke Ave. W: Overview Map C2

UV

Union St.: Overview Map E4; Map 2 C4; Map 3 F6

E Union St.: Map 4 F3

Union Bay Pl. NE: Map 6 A5

University Bridge: Map 6 C1

University St.: Map 2 C4; Map 3 F6

University Way N: Map 6 A2

Valley St.: Map 3 C2, C5

E Valley St.: Map 4 C4, C6

View Mont Way W: Overview Map C1

Vine St.: Map 3 F3

Virginia St.: Map 2 B2; Map 3 F5

WXY

Wall St.: Map 3 E3

Walla Walla Rd.: Map 6 A4, B4

Wallingford Ave.: Map 5 A5, B5

Ward Pl. N: Map 3 C3

Ward St.: Map 3 C2, C5

E Ward St.: Map 4 B4, B6

Warren Ave. N: Map 3 A2, B2, C2, E2; Map 5 E2

Warren Pl.: Map 3 B2

S Washington St.: Map 1 B3

Waverly Pl. N: Map 3 A4

S Weller St.: Map 1 C5

Welmore St.: Map 7

Western Ave.: Map 1 A2; Map 2 B1, D3; Map 3 F3

Westlake Ave.: Map 2 A3; Map 3 A4, D4

Westlake Ave. N: Map 5 F4

Wheeler St.: Map 5 F3

Whitman Ave. N: Map 5 A3, C3

Whitman Ct.: Map 6 A4

Williams Ave. W: Map 7

Winslow Pl. N: Map 5 B3

Woodland Park Ave.: Map 5 A3, D3

Woodlawn Ave. N: Map 5 A4, B4

Yale Ave.: Map 3 E6

Yale Ave. E: Map 3 A6; Map 5 F6

Yale Ave. N: Map 3 C6, D6

Yale Pl. E: Map 3 A6

Yale Ter.: Map 5 F6

Yesler Way: Overview Map E5; Map 1 A3; Map 2 F4

INDEX

AB

A Contemporary Theatre (ACT): 67

Allen, Paul: 10

Annex Theatre: 72

Argosy Cruises: 4, 73, 77

arts and leisure: XIV, 59-78

Asian American community: VII

Bainbridge Island: 7, 8

Ballard: Map 7, 17; nightlife 43-44; restaurants 33; shops 57-58; sights 17-18

Ballard Fetherston Gallery: 64

ballet: 68

bars: see nightlife

beauty salons: see shops

Belltown/Queen Anne: Map 3; hotels 83-84; museums and galleries 63-64; nightlife 38-40; performing arts 68-70; recreation 74-75; restaurants 24-28; shops 51-52; sights 8-11

Benaroya Hall: 67

Benham Gallery: 59, 62

best: hotels 79; museums and galleries 59; nightlife 35; of Seattle itinerary X-XI; performing arts 59; recreation 73; restaurants 19; shops 45; sights 1

bicycling in Seattle: XII

Bite of Seattle: 90

Bon-Macy's Holiday Parade: 90

Book-It Repertory Theatre: 68

bookstores: see shops

Bremerton: 7

Broadway Performance Hall: 70

Bryan Ohno Gallery: 60

Bumbershoot: VIII, 90

Burke-Gilman Trail: XIII, 75

Burke Museum of Natural History and Culture: XII, 1, 14

buses: 88

business hours: 89

C

Capitol Hill: Map 4; hotels 85-86; museums and galleries 64-65; nightlife 40-42; performing arts 70-71; recreation 75; restaurants 28-30; shops 52-53; sights 11-12

Carolyn Staley Fine Prints: 60

Center for Wooden Boats, The: 63

Center on Contemporary Art (CoCA): 63

Central Library: XI, 1, 3

Chateau Ste. Michelle winery: 14, 70

Children's Museum, The: 63

Chinatown Discovery Tours: 78

clothing shops: *see* shops

Coast Guard Museum Northwest: 60

coffeehouses: 29

Columbia Winery: 14

comedy: *see* performing arts

communications: 92

concerts: *see* nightlife, performing arts, summer concert series

Consolidated Works: 68

convention and visitors bureau: 89

D

dance clubs: *see* nightlife

Davidson Galleries: 60

Daybreak Star Indian Cultural Center: 18

day trips: 14

Dimitriou's Jazz Alley: 59, 68

disabled access: 91

Discovery Park: XIII, 1, 18

downtown: Map 2; hotels 80-82; museums and galleries 62-63; nightlife 36-37; performing arts 67-68; recreation 73-74; restaurants 21-24; shops 47-50; sights 3-8

driving: 87-88

dry cleaners: 92

EF

Earshot Jazz Festival: 90

Egyptian Theatre: 71

emergency services: 91

events: 89

Experience Music Project: XI, 1, 8, 10

farms (pick your own): 14

festivals: 89

5th Avenue Theatre, The: 59, 67

First Thursday Gallery Walks: 62

Flury & Company, Ltd.: 60

food stores: *see* shops

Foolproof for the Performing Arts: 72

Foster Island Walk: 76

Foster/White Gallery: XIV, 59, 60, 61

Fourth of July: 90

Fremont Fair: 90

Fremont Public Art Walk: XV, 75

Fremont/Wallingford: Map 5; hotels 86; museums and galleries 65; nightlife 42-43; recreation 75-76; restaurants 30-31; shops 54-56; sights 13

Frye Art Museum: 65

G

galleries: *see* museums and galleries

Gas Works Park: XIII, 59, 76

getaway hotels: 84

G. Gibson Gallery: 61

Grand Illusion Cinema, The: 72

Green Lake Park: XII, 77

Gregg's Green Lake Cycle: XII, 77

Greg Kucera Gallery: 61

Grover/Thurston Gallery: 59, 61, 62

grunge history: 39

H

Harborview Medical Center: 91

Harvard-Belmont Historic District: 12

health and emergency services: 91

Henry Art Gallery: 59, 65

Hing Hay Park: 73

Hiram M. Chittenden Locks: XIII, 1, 17

History House: 65

history: VIII

hotels: 79-86; *see also* Hotels Index

Howard House: 61

IJK

IMAX theaters: 6, 10

Interbay Golf Center: 77

International District: VII; *see also* Pioneer Square/International District

Internet: 92

Intiman Theatre: 68

introduction: VI

itineraries: X-XV; best of Seattle X-XI; Seattle by bike XII; artistic Seattle XIV

Japanese Garden: 16

jazz: *see* performing arts

Kenmore Air: 74

Kerry Park: 59, 75

Key Arena: 68

Klondike Gold Rush National Historic Park: 2

LM

Lake Union Houseboats: 76

Lake View Cemetery: XIV, 12

LGBT Pride Parade and Celebration: 90

Linda Hodges Gallery: 61, 62

live music clubs: *see* nightlife

local designers: 50

Madison Park: 53

Magnuson Park/Art Walk: 78

Marion Oliver Mccaw Hall: 59, 68

Martin-Zambito Fine Art: 64

Meany Hall for the Performing Arts: 71

media: 91

Missy Morrisey: 50

monorail: *see* Seattle Center Monorail

Moore Theatre, The: 67

movie houses: *see* performing arts

multiuse venues: *see* performing arts

Museum of History & Industry (MOHAI): 62, 65

museums and galleries: 60-66

music scene: VIII, 39

N

National Fallen Firefighters Memorial: 2

New Year's Eve at the Space Needle: 90

nightlife: 35-44; *see also* Nightlife Index

911 Media Arts Center: 69

Nordic Heritage Museum: 66

North Beach: 18

Northwest Asian American Theatre (NWAAT): 67

Northwest Film Forum: 71

Northwest Folklife
Festival: 89
NW Outdoor Center:
75, 77

OP

Odyssey Maritime
Discovery
Center: 66
On the Boards: 69
opera: 68
Pacific Northwest cui-
sine: 27
Pacific Science
Center: 1, 9
Paramount
Theatre: 68
parking: 88
performing arts:
67-72
pharmacies: 91
Phoenix Rishing
Gallery: 50
Pike Place Market: X,
Map 2, 1, 4
Pioneer Square
Historic District:
X, 1, 2
Pioneer Square/
International
District: Map 1;
hotels 80; muse-
ums and galleries
60-62; nightlife
36; performing
arts 67; recreation
73; restaurants
20-21; shops 46;
sights 2-3
public transporta-
tion: 88

QR

Queen Anne: see
Belltown/Queen
Anne
queer bars and clubs:
see nightlife,
Map 4
Ravenna Park: 59, 78
Re-Bar: 69
recreation: 73-78
Remlinger Farms: 14
renting a car: 87-88
restaurants: 19-
34; see also
Restaurants Index
Ride the Ducks: 75
Roq La Rue
Gallery: 64

S

Safeco Field: 73
safety: 91
Science Fiction
Museum and Hall
of Fame: 10, 64
Seafair: 90
Seattle Aquarium: 1, 5

Seattle Architecture
Foundation
Tours: 73
Seattle Art Museum:
XIV, 1, 6-7, 62
Seattle Asian Art
Museum: XIV, 1,
11, 65
Seattle Center
Monorail: IX, 88
Seattle Children's
Theatre: 69
Seattle Cinerama
Theatre: 59, 69
Seattle Festival of
Improv Theater: 89
Seattle International
Children's
Festival: 89
Seattle International
Film Festival: 89
Seattle Metropolitan
Police Museum: 61
Seattle Public
Theater: 72
Seattle Repertory
Theatre: 70
Seattle-Tacoma
Airport: 87
See Seattle Walking
Tours: 74
self-guided tours: see
itineraries
Shilshole Bay
Marina: 78
shops: 45-58; see
also Shops Index
sights: 1-18
Skagit Valley Tulip
Festival: 14
Smith Tower: 3
smoking: 92
Solstice Parade and
Fremont Fair: 90
Soundbridge: 62
South Beach: 18
Space Needle: XI, 1, 10
spas: see shops
St. Mark's Episcopal
Cathedral: 71
Starbucks: 29
summer concert
series: 70
Summer Nights
at South Lake
Union: 70
Swedish Medical
Center: 91

TU

Taproot Theatre: 72
taxis: 88
Teatro Zinzanni: 70
Theater
Schmeater: 71
theater: see perform-
ing arts
Tillicum Village: 74

tipping: 92
Town Hall Seattle: 68
Underground Tour: X,
59, 73
University District
Public Art Tour: 76
University District:
Map 6, 15; hotels
86; museums and
galleries 65; night-
life 43; performing
arts 71; recreation
76-77; restaurants
31-33; shops 56-
57; sights 14-16
University of
Washington
Medical Center: 91
University of
Washington
Waterfront
Activities
Center: 77
University of
Washington: XII,
Map 6, 16

VW

Velocity Dance
Center: 71
Virginia Mason: 91
visitor informa-
tion: 89
Volunteer Park:
XIV, 75
walking tours: 73, 74,
75, 76, 78
Wallingford: see
Fremont/
Wallingford
Washington Park
Arboretum: 1, 15
Washington State
Ferries: X, 1, 7-
8, 77
water activities: 77
Waterfall Garden
Park: 2, 73
Waterfront Park:
4, 74
Waterfront Streetcar:
X, 74
waterfront: Map 2, 4
weather: 89
Willard Smith
Planetarium: 10
wineries: 14
Wing Luke Asian
Museum: 62
Winterfest: 90
Woodland Park Rose
Garden: 76
Woodland Park Zoo:
XIII, 1, 13, 70
Woodside-Braseth
Gallery: 63
World's Fair: IX

RESTAURANTS INDEX

Agua Verde Paddle Club & Cafe: XII, 31
Alexandria's on Second: 21
Apartment Bistro: 24
Assaggio Ristorante: 24
Asteroid Cafe: 30
Baguette Box: XIV, 28
Bandoleone: 30
Bauhaus Books & Coffee: 28
Brasa: 24
Brooklyn Seafood, Steak & Oyster House: 4, 21
Cafe Besalu: 33
Cafe Flora: 34
Café Lago: 32
Café Paloma: 20
Campagne: 19, 21
Canlis: 34
Cascadia Restaurant: 19, 24
Cedars: 32
Chez Shea: 19, 22
China Gate: 20
Crave: 29
Crow: 19, 22
Dahlia Lounge: 25
Dandelion: 33
Earth & Ocean: 22
El Gaucho: 25

El Greco: 29
Flying Fish: XV, 19, 25
The Georgian: 22
Grand Central Baking Company: X, 20
The Harvest Vine: 34
Hattie's Hat: XIII, 33
Hilltop Ale House: 25
Jai Thai: 30
Kabul Afghan Cuisine: 31
Kingfish Cafe: 29
Lampreia: 25
Le Pichet: 22
The Library Bistro: 22
Lola: 19, 26
Macrina Bakery & Cafe: 26
Mamounia: 29
Maneki: 20
Market Street Grill: 33
Matt's in the Market: 23
Metropolitan Grill: 23
Mistral: 19, 26
Monsoon: 30
Oceanaire Seafood Room: 23
Osteria La Spiga: 30
Ototo Sushi: 26
Palisade: 34
Pan Africa: 23

Place Pigalle: 23
Ray's Boathouse: 19, 34, 77
Restaurant Zoë: 26
Rover's: 19, 34
Roxy's Deli: 31
Saito's Japanese Café & Bar: 27
Salumi: 20
Sapphire Kitchen & Bar: 27
Sazerac: 23
Serafina: 27
Shanghai Garden: 20
Shiro's: 27
Sky City: XI, 10, 28
Takohachi: 21
Tango: 30
Teahouse Kuan Yin: 31
Thaiku: 17, 33
Than Brothers: 15, 32
35th St. Bistro: 31
Troiani: 23
Tup Tim Thai: 28
Ugly Mug Cafe: 32
Union Bay Cafe: 33
Waterfront: 28
Wild Ginger: 19, 24
Zeitgeist Coffee: XI, 21

NIGHTLIFE INDEX

Bad Juju Lounge: 40
Bada Lounge: XV, 35, 36
The Baltic Room: 40
Barça: 40
Beso del Sol: 42
Big Time Brewery & Alehouse: 15, 43
Blue Moon Tavern: 43
BluWater Bistro: 38
Café Venus and the Mars Bar: 38
The Capitol Club: 40
Catwalk Club: 36
Century Ballroom: 40
Cha Cha Lounge: 35, 40
Chapel: 35, 41
Chop Suey: 41
Club Medusa: 38
Contour: 36

The Crocodile Café: 38, 39
Cyclops: 38
Element: 35, 38
Fabulous Buckaroo Tavern: 42
Fenix Underground: 36
Garage: 41
The George & Dragon Pub: 43
Graceland: 39
Linda's Tavern: 39, 41
Manray: 41
Marcus' Martini Heaven: 36
Mirabeau Room: 39
Neighbours: 35, 42
Neumos: 36
Nitelite: 36
Old Town Alehouse: 35, 43

The People's Pub: 44
The Pink Door: XI, 37
Portalis: 17, 44
Rendezvous: 39
Shorty's Coney Island: 39
The Showbox: 37, 39
Sunset Tavern: 44
Tini Bigs: 35, 39
Tommy's Nightclub: 43
Tost: 43
Tractor Tavern: 44
Triangle Lounge: 43
Triple Door: XV, 37
Tula's Restaurant and Nightclub: 40
Virginia Inn: 37
The Wildrose: 42
Zig Zag Café: 37

SHOPS INDEX

Archie McPhee: 17, 57
Bailey/Coy Books: 52
Ballard: 17, 57
Barnes & Noble: 56
Bert's Red Apple Market: 53
Bitters Co.: 54
Borders Books and Music: 47
Bud's Jazz Records: 46
Bulldog News: 15, 56
Burnt Sugar: 54
Cactus: 53
Camelion Design: 57
Capitol Hill: XIV, 52
Chartreuse International: 51
Cookin: 53
Dandelion Botanical Company: 54
Deluxe Junk: 45, 54
Edie's: 53
Elliott Bay Book Company: 46
Enexile: 54
Essenza: 54
Fini: 47
Fireworks Gallery: 45, 46
Flora and Henri: 47
Fox's Gem Shop: 47
Fran's Chocolates: 56
Fremont: XIII, 54
Gasworks Park Kite Shop: 54
Habitude at the Locks: 58

Isadora's Antiques: 48
Jeri Rice: 48
J. Gilbert Footwear: 48
Kinokuniya Book Store: 46
La Femme: 51
Laguna Vintage Pottery: 45, 46
Left Bank Books Collective: 48
Les Amis: 55
Lipstick Traces: 53
Lola Pop: 55
Lucca Great Finds: 58
Luly Yang: 50
M Coy Books: 48
Mercer: 56
Metsker Maps of Seattle: 48
Nordstrom: XI, 48
Olivine Atelier: 45, 58
Open Books: A Poem Emporium: 55
Opus 204: 48
Original Children's Shop: 53
Pacific Place: XI, 45, 49
Parfumerie Elizabeth George: 49
Ped: 45, 49
Pike Place Market: 49
Pretty Parlor: 58
Queen Anne: 51
Queen Anne Books: 51

Queen Anne Mail & Dispatch: 51
Red Light: 53
REI: 53
Rhinestone Rosie: 45, 52
A Salon Day Spa Boutique: 52
Scandinavian Gift Shop: 58
Seattle Caviar Company: 56
Secret Garden Bookshop: 58
The Soap Box: 56
Sonic Boom Records: 45, 55
Spa del Lago: 53
Sway & Cake: 49
The Teacup: 52
Tsue Chong Co.: 46
Tulip: 49
Twist: 50
Ummelina: 50
University Book Store: 57
University Village: 57
Uwajimaya: 45, 46
Wallingford Center: 55
White Horse: 50
Wide World Books & Maps: 45, 56
Yankee Peddler: 53
Ye Olde Curiosity Shop: 4, 50
Zebraclub: 50

HOTELS INDEX

Alexis Hotel: 79, 80

The Bacon Mansion Bed & Breakfast: 85

Best Western Pioneer Square Hotel: 80

Best Western University Tower Hotel: 86

Capitol Hill Inn: 85

College Inn: 86

The Edgewater: 79, 83

Fairmont Olympic Hotel: 80

Gaslight Inn: 85

Grand Hyatt Seattle: 80

Hill House Bed and Breakfast: 85

Hotel Ändra: 79, 83

Hotel Monaco: 80

Hotel Vintage Park: 80

Inn at Harbor Steps: 81

Inn at the Market: 81

MarQueen Hotel: 83

Mayflower Park Hotel: 81

Mediterranean Inn: 83

Mildred's Bed & Breakfast: 85

Panama Hotel: 79, 80

The Paramount Hotel: 81

Pensione Nichols: 81

Renaissance Seattle Hotel: 82

The Roosevelt Hotel: 82

Salisbury House: 85

Salish Lodge & Spa: 84

Seattle Marriott Waterfront: 82

Sheraton Seattle Hotel and Towers: 82

Silver Cloud Inn – Lake Union: 83

Sorrento Hotel: 79, 86

Summerfield Suites by Wyndham: 82

Vance Hotel: 83

W Hotel: 82

Warwick Hotel: 84

Watertown: 86

The Westin Seattle: 84

Willows Lodge: 84

The Woodmark Hotel on Lake Washington: 84

CONTRIBUTORS TO THE SECOND EDITION

PATRICIA CAMPBELL   *Sights, Side Walks, Recreation*
Patricia Campbell is a freelance writer whose family settled in Washington Territory around 1860. A Pacific Northwest history enthusiast with a background in theater, Patty shares her local expertise with national travel guides and moonlights for several entertainment publications.

JESSICA DAVIS   *City Essentials*
Jessica Davis has written for more than 20 newspapers in the Seattle area, including the *Seattle Post-Intelligencer*. She was born and raised in the Seattle area and has lived there for most of her life.

KRISTINE EKMAN   *Hotels*
Born and raised in Seattle, Kristine Ekman has written for many local Northwest publications. Even though she has shopped in the Marrakech bazaar and waited for goat herders on Norwegian one-lane roads, the scenic beauty of the Puget Sound keeps calling her back.

LYNN MARSHALL   *Restaurants*
A native of the Seattle area, Lynn Marshall is the Northwest Bureau Researcher for the *Los Angeles Times* and spends as much free time as she can cooking, eating, and writing about food.

NICOLE MEOLI   *Shops*
Nicole Meoli is a freelance writer/editor living in Seattle. She was most recently editor in chief of *Where Magazine* in San Francisco, where she wrote a monthly fashion column and oversaw annual fashion issues of the magazine.

RYAN SIMANTEL   *Introduction, A Day in Seattle, Neighborhoods, Sights Callouts, Nightlife, Museums and Galleries*
Ryan Simantel is primarily a Seattle-based entertainment reporter and photographer for America Online. Although his other accomplishments include earning a degree in English with honors from UW and contributing to several prominent Northwest publications, he started out just like many others do in Seattle – as a barista for Starbucks.

JANET WILSON   *Performing Arts, Nightlife – Live Music Venues*
Janet Wilson is a deejay at KIXI AM 880 in Bellevue. She also writes the KIXI calendar and emcees the occasional concert. A self-professed daydreamer, Janet has lived in the Seattle area since 1984.

CONTRIBUTORS TO THE FIRST EDITION
Roberta Cruger, Sara Dickerman, Val Mallinson, Kathy Schultz

PHOTO CREDITS

ELLIE BEHRSTOCK: Map 4 Garage; Page 28 El Greco.

RYAN SIMANTEL: Page 3 Central Library; Page 6 Washington State Ferries; page 13 Harvard-Belmont District; page 32 Than Brothers; page 38 Cyclops; Page 42 Neumos; Page 47 Laguna Vintage Pottery; Page 49 Jeri Rice; Page 74 Waterfront Streetcar; Page 81 Hotel Vintage Park; Page 85 The Beacon Mansion Bed and Breakfast, Capitol Hill Inn.

JASON GRIEGO: Page 8 Experience Music Project; Page 49 Metsker Maps of Seattle; Page 57 Bulldog news; Page 64 Experience Music Project; Page 69 Re-Bar.

All other photos by Phil Shipman

MOON METRO SEATTLE
2ND EDITION

Avalon Publishing,
An Imprint of Avalon Publishing Group, Inc.

Text and maps © 2005 by Avalon Travel Publishing

Transit System Map courtesy King County Metro Transit, September 2004

ISBN: 1-56691-894-4
ISSN: 1541-8898

Editor and Series Manager: Grace Fujimoto
Design: Jacob Goolkasian
Map Design: Mike Morgenfeld, Suzanne Service
Production Coordinator: Darren Alessi
Graphics Coordinators: Justin Marler, Deborah Dutcher
Cartographer: Suzanne Service
Map Editor: Kat Smith
Copy Editor: Mia Lipman
Fact Checkers: Jessica Davis, Sabrina Young
Front cover photos: Smaller image: Donna Day/Photodisc/Getty Images;
Larger image: C. McIntyre/PhotoLink/Getty Images

Printed in China through Colorcraft Ltd., Hong Kong
Printing History
1st edition – 2003
2nd edition – July 2005
5 4 3 2 1

Please send all feedback about this book to:

Moon Metro Seattle
Avalon Travel Publishing
1400 65th Street, Suite 250
Emeryville, CA 94608, USA
email: atpfeedback@avalonpub.com
website: www.moon.com

MOON METRO

- AMSTERDAM
- BARCELONA
- BERLIN
- BOSTON
- CHICAGO
- LAS VEGAS
- LONDON
- LOS ANGELES
- MIAMI
- MONTRÉAL
- NEW YORK CITY
- PARIS
- ROME
- SAN FRANCISCO
- SEATTLE
- TORONTO
- VANCOUVER
- WASHINGTON D.C.

AVAILABLE AT YOUR FAVORITE BOOK AND TRAVEL STORES

www.moon.com

UNFOLD THE CITY

UNFOLD THE CITY

UNFOLD
MOON METRO
LONDON

"A SLEEK TWO-IN-ONE BLEND OF ADVICE AND STREET MAPS."
—U.S. NEWS & WORLD REPORT

MOON METRO
CHICAGO

"A SLEEK TWO-IN-ONE BLEND OF ADVICE AND STREET MAPS."
—U.S. NEWS & WORLD REPORT

MOON METRO
WASHINGTON D.C.

"A SLEEK TWO-IN-ONE BLEND OF ADVICE AND STREET MAPS."
—U.S. NEWS & WORLD REPORT